CITIZENSHIP AND THE CHALLENGE OF GLOBAL EDUCATION

CITIZENSHIP AND THE CHALLENGE OF GLOBAL EDUCATION

Audrey Osler and Kerry Vincent

Trentham Books
Stoke on Trent, UK and Sterling, USA

Trentham Books Limited

Westview House	22883 Quicksilver Drive
734 London Road	Sterling
Oakhill	VA 20166-2012
Stoke on Trent	USA
Staffordshire	
England ST4 5NP	

© 2002 Audrey Osler and Kerry Vincent

First published 2002

British Library Cataloguing-in-Publication Data
A catalogue record for this book is available from the British Library

1 85856 268 6

Designed and typeset by Trentham Print Design Ltd., Chester and printed in Great Britain by Cromwell Press Ltd., Wiltshire.

CONTENTS

Acknowledgements

We wish to thank a number of individuals and organisations that supported us in the writing of this book:

The European Commission for its support of the *Comenius Thematic Network on Global Education* (71552-CP-1999-I-BE-Comenius-C2). This permitted us to attend meetings in Budapest and Athens during 2001 and to participate in discussions with colleagues on global education. It also enabled us to carry out a study of institutional support for global education in four EU countries: Denmark, England, the Republic of Ireland and the Netherlands.

The European Federation for Intercultural Learning and Alessio Surian for co-ordinating the Thematic Network on Global Education.

Core members of the Network:
- Council of Europe North South Centre
- Open Learning Centre (Bulgaria)
- National Innovative Centre for General Education (SPF) (Denmark)
- Hellenic Association of Educators for Environmental Education (Greece)
- Centre for Citizenship Studies in Education (CCSE), University of Leicester (UK)
- Centre for Global Education (UK)
- Centrum voor Mondiaal Onderwijs (CMO) (Netherlands)
- National Committee for International Co-operation and Sustainable Development (NCDO) (Netherlands).

We are very appreciative of the support given to us by colleagues.

At the Centre for Citizenship Studies in Education:
Barbara Hall, Samantha Keenan and Margaret Stace for administrative support and assistance in preparing the manuscript.

Hugh Starkey for attending a Thematic Network meeting, for comments on drafts and especially for discussions and ideas which have informed our thinking. Chris Wilkins for representing CCSE in the Thematic Network on Global Education and for reading draft chapters.

Other participants in Network meetings in Budapest and Athens:
Cesar Birzea, Margot Brown, Poul Erik Christofferson, Astrit Dautaj, Dakmara Georgescu, Helle Jarlmose, Gerard Lommerse, Vasillis Psallidas, Tzonka Ilieva Renarova, Harry de Ridder, Claudette Salmon, Miguel Silva, Carsten Skjoldborg, Rumen Valchev, Liam Wegimont, Virginia Valova.

Grateful thanks to all others who responded to our requests for information:
Douglas Bourn, Frances Burns, Filomena Cassis, Ana Cotrim, Carsten Djursaa, Hans Hooghoff, Debbie Kenny, Marianne Kleist, Babs de Klerk, Neils Larsen, Stephen McCarthy, Ida McDonnell, Grainne O'Byrne, Colm O'Cuanachain, Hilary O'Cuanachain, Karen O'Shea, Birte Ravn, Johnny Sheehan, Scott Sinclair, Jørn Søgaard, Mariëtte van Stalborch, Isobel Tamen, Thomas Tichelmann.

ACRONYMS AND ABBREVIATIONS

ASPnet   UNESCO Associated Schools Project

CCSE   Centre for Citizenship Studies in Education

CDU   Curriculum Development Unit (Ireland)

CDVEC   City of Dublin Vocational Education Committee

CENESA Co-operation in Education between the Netherlands and South Africa programme

CITO   National Institute for Educational Measurement (Netherlands)

CMO   Centre for Global Education (Netherlands)

CPD   Continuing Professional Development

CRC   UN Convention on the Rights of the Child

CSPE   Civic Social and Political Education (Ireland)

DAN   Direct Action Network (USA)

DANIDA Danish Co-operation for Environment and Development Agency

DE   Development Education

DEA   Development Education Association

DEAG   Development Education Action Group (Ireland)

DEC   Development Education Centre

DEFRA   Department for the Environment, Food and Rural Affairs

DEFY   Development Education for Youth (Ireland)

DES   Department for Education and Science (Ireland)

DETR   Department of the Environment, Transport and the Regions

DfEE   Department for Education and Employment, now DfES

DfES   Department for Education and Skills

DFID   Department for International Development

DOOR   Project to promote ESD (Netherlands)

EA   Equality Authority (Ireland)

EC European Community

EE Environmental Education

EPA European Parents' Association

ESD Education for Sustainable Development

ESRC Economic and Social Research Council

EU European Union

FORUM Institute for Multicultural Development (Netherlands)

GDP Gross Domestic Product

GE Global Education

GLADE Centre for Global and Development Education

GLOBE Global Learning and Observations to Benefit the Environment (Netherlands)

HRE Human Rights Education

ICDU In-Career Development Unit (Ireland)

ICT Information and Communications Technology

IEA International Association for the Evaluation of Educational Achievement

IICD International Institute for Communication and Development (Netherlands)

IMF International Monetary Fund

IPP Centre for Political Participation (Netherlands)

LEA Local Education Authority

LSC Learning and Skills Council

LSO National Agency for Global Education (Netherlands)

MS Danish Association for International Co-operation

MUNGA Model United Nations General Assembly

NCCA National Council for Curriculum Assessment (Ireland)

NCCRI National Consultative Committee on Racism and Interculturalism (Ireland)

NCDE National Committee for Development Education (Ireland)

NCDO National Committee for International Co-operation (Netherlands)

NFER National Foundation for Educational Research

NGFL   National Grid for Learning

NGO   Non-Governmental Organisation

NODE   Network of Grassroots in Development Education (Ireland)

NSC   North-South Centre of the Council of Europe

ODA   Overseas Development Aid

OECD   Organisation for Economic Co-operation and Development

OFSTED Office for Standards in Education

PSHE   Personal Social and Health Education

QCA   Qualifications and Curriculum Authority

RAXEN European Information Network on Racism and Xenophobia

SLO   Netherlands Institute for Curriculum Development

SPF   National Innovative Centre of General Education (Denmark)

SPHE   Social Personal and Health Education (Ireland)

TST   ASPnet Transatlantic Slave Trade Project

TTA   Teacher Training Agency

UDHR   Universal Declaration of Human Rights

UK   United Kingdom

UN   United Nations

UNESCO United Nations Educational, Scientific and Cultural Organisation

UNICEF United Nations International Children's Emergency Fund

US   United States

VEC   Vocational Education Committee (Ireland)

WTO   World Trade Organisation

Foreword

Glenys Kinnock MEP

Global education has a critical part to play in providing a political response to the process of globalisation. It is about enabling people – young people in particular – to understand the link between their own lives, and those of other people throughout the world.

As a teacher of young children for many years, I have always been committed to the importance of teaching how to value others and their experiences – both globally and locally. A global citizen should appreciate diversity and should be keen to take action in the interests of others.

It is clear now – more than ever before – that there is a need to understand the nature of international politics, and the realities of interdependence. It is vital for everyone to be given the chance to participate in an increasingly globalised world. Issues relating to global citizenship, human rights, sustainability and security need to be better understood, and, as Professor Osler convincingly argues, should be a central component of every student's curriculum.

This book is a clear acknowledgement of the fact that there is a growing consensus that we have to prepare people for living in an increasingly global world. Trends in world trade and investment, travel and communications have brought us closer together than ever before. Through the window of the television, or on the Internet, we can watch the world evolve. At the same time, power is being concentrated in fewer and fewer hands, and there is a sense of powerlessness and helplessness, and we are not sure how to shape an effective agenda. The central irony that we face is that despite a growing trend towards internationalism, ordinary citizens express their disquiet about their inability to control, or even influence, what happens in the world.

How we deal with this has fundamental implications for education. Few young people or adults have a basic understanding of the social structures and the processes which shape their lives. Few have a theoretical or practical understanding of their rights or respon-sibilities, and few have a considered view on how these can be applied and extended in order to resolve social problems and create a 'better' world. Audrey Osler and Kerry Vincent's case studies offer an insightful look at what is being done by governments, local authorities, schools and NGOs to address these concerns.

The events of September 11th, the subsequent military action in Afghanistan and recent developments in the Middle East, all bring a new sense of urgency to this debate. We now know that even the most powerful nation on earth can't defend itself from a bunch of determined fanatics. We also know that there are clear links between international terrorism, drugs, extremism and the proliferation of arms. We face many moral and ethical questions but also there are fundamental challenges and threats to our planet, and all its people. In this context, Professor Osler persuasively demonstrates that educating our citizens about fundamental human rights and respect for others is vital. In response to the threats of racism and prejudice, education for global citizenship in a multi-ethnic context is crucial. Ours is a world of inequalities.

Worldwide, 1.2 billion people live on less than a dollar a day, and the current patterns of global growth mean that we will simply not reach the internationally agreed development target - of halving the number of people living in poverty by 2015. At the same time it is shocking to note that the annual revenue of General Motors exceeds the gross national product of 45 African countries, and in Mexico 24 individuals possess more wealth than 24 million of their fellow citizens.

Poverty is a man-made disease which scars the whole of our planet. If we ever needed to learn the lessons about the implications of neglecting the need to tackle poverty it is now. Whilst poverty can never excuse terrorism, it can explain why human beings are recruited to terrorism. It breeds disease, ignorance, inequality, instability, intolerance, privation, division and war.

I believe that our task, therefore, is to globalise social progress. There needs to be a response to the aspirations of people everywhere for decent and productive jobs in conditions of freedom, equality, security and human dignity. As citizens, we have a responsibility to inform ourselves and press for greater understanding of the nature of development, and the need for growth with equality. That means understanding complex issues, but the effective campaigns against debt, and for arms control, prove that this is not an impediment to progress. These campaigns prove that people will grapple with a lot of technical detail if they believe that there is an important case to be made. Armed with the right information, committed citizens believe that they have influence, and that they can change the world. Whether it is a sponsored bike ride for Nicaragua, or lighting a candle for peace, or running a marathon for Mozambique, many of us work in different ways to open people's eyes, ears and hearts.

Perversely, developed societies – like our own – appear to be under growing pressure to look inwards. The shaving of overseas aid budgets in several industrialised countries in recent years is just one symptom of this widespread rejection of an international perspective – although targets have now been set by many countries to reverse this trend. Such a blinkered view is not only a matter of moral regret, it is dangerously myopic in an age in which the fortunes, and misfortunes, of nations are more intimately linked than ever before. Common sense alone tells us that some issues are of such diversity and dimension that they simply cannot be dealt with by governments acting alone, or even several governments acting in concert. The principles which we hold dear cannot be applied at home and ignored elsewhere. We need to understand that dealing with national issues of fairness, equality and liberty also requires, by necessity, that we look outwards.

Audrey Osler's erudite analysis provides us with crucial lessons for the future, and it provides all of us who lobby and campaign on these issues with a better understanding of the critical importance of global citizenship. This book also galvanises us to insist that decision-makers at every level, both North and South, should prioritise the need to educate their citizens about globalisation.

The task ahead is formidable but we have to build into future generations a determination to grapple with indifference, and instil the political will to demand real change. As Nelson Mandela once said, 'Our common humanity transcends the oceans and all national boundaries.... Let it never be asked of any of us – what did we do when we knew that another was oppressed?'

1
Introduction

This book is aimed at teachers, student teachers and teacher educators responsible for developing citizenship education programmes. It will also be of interest to researchers and policy-makers who are interested in comparative and international education policy.

Teachers face a number of challenges in preparing their students for citizenship within a fast-changing world. In particular, they face the challenge of teaching for equity, justice and solidarity in contexts where their students are all too aware of inequality and injustice, both in their own communities and in the wider world. Education for citizenship, like all other aspects of education, needs to take account of our global interdependence. Processes of globalisation make this task particularly urgent.

In this book we are concerned with strategies, policies and plans which prepare young people for living together in an interdependent world. These aspects of education are sometimes referred to internationally as global education or education for peace, democracy and human rights. The draft Global Education Charter of the Council of Europe's North South Centre defines global education as education which encourages learners 'to identify links between the local, the regional and the world-wide level and to address inequality'. We maintain that global education is characterised by pedagogical approaches based on human rights and a concern for social justice which encourage critical thinking and responsible participation. Global education covers:

Education for human rights, peace, international understanding, tolerance and non-violence. It also [includes] all aspects of education relating to the principles of democracy and multicultural and inter-cultural education (UNESCO, 2000).

Global education also requires education for sustainable development (UNESCO, 1995). We therefore include, within our review of global education initiatives, the global dimensions of development education and environmental education. Some aspects of global education may be addressed through established curriculum subjects and others are likely to be addressed through special projects.

GLOBAL EDUCATION

Aim
To build a global culture of peace through the promotion of values, attitudes and behaviour which enable the realisation of democracy, development and human rights.

Definition
Global education encompasses the strategies, policies and plans that prepare young people and adults for living together in an interdependent world. It is based on the principles of co-operation, non-violence, respect for human rights and cultural diversity, democracy and tolerance. It is characterised by pedagogical approaches based on human rights and a concern for social justice which encourage critical thinking and responsible participation. Learners are encouraged to make links between local, regional and world-wide issues and to address inequality.

Citizenship and the Challenge of Global Education considers why global education is critical and how it might be realised. It examines ways in which institutional support for global education has developed in four countries in Western Europe and draws lessons from these experiences. Increasingly, in many countries, citizenship education programmes are being recognised as a key means by which global education can be mainstreamed, so as to support and enable the development of societies and communities based on peace, democracy and human rights.

These concerns have long been on the agenda of international organisations such as UNESCO and of regional inter-governmental organisations such as the Council of Europe. Indeed, UNESCO was set up as part of a project for world peace. So Ministers of Education meeting at the 44th session of the UNESCO's International Conference on Education in 1994 in Geneva, mindful of their responsibilities in this field, determined:

> to strive resolutely ... to take suitable steps to establish in educational institutions an atmosphere contributing to the success of education for international understanding, so that they become ideal places for the exercise of tolerance, respect for human rights, the practice of democracy and learning about the diversity and wealth of cultural identities (UNESCO, 1995: 2.2).

Accordingly, the following year the General Conference of UNESCO approved an *Integrated Framework of Action on Education for Peace, Human Rights and Democracy* at its 28th session in Paris, which identified policies and actions to be taken at institutional, national and international levels to realise such education. It states:

> There must be education for peace, human rights and democracy. It cannot, however, be restricted to specialised subjects and knowledge. The whole of education must transmit this message and the atmosphere of the institution must be in harmony with the application of democratic standards (UNESCO: 1995: IV. 17).

The intention is that education for peace, human rights and democracy should be a mainstream concern and part of the entitlement of every learner. The UNESCO General Conference recognised that any attempt to incorporate these issues into the curriculum will need to be matched by processes of democratisation within education authorities and schools. The UNESCO statement echoes the sentiment of the Council of Europe Committee of Ministers Recommendation some ten years earlier, on teaching and learning about human rights:

> Democracy is best learned in a democratic setting where participation is encouraged, where views can be expressed openly and discussed, where there is freedom of expression for pupils and teachers,

3

and where there is fairness and justice. An appropriate climate is, therefore, an essential complement to effective learning about human rights (Council of Europe, 1985, re-printed in Osler and Starkey, 1996).

Nevertheless, such statements are likely to remain at the level of exhortation, unless opportunities are created for national policy-makers, education authorities, schools and teachers to explore the meanings of these documents in depth and devise action strategies at each level through to the classroom. It is only when such (democratic) processes are set up that education for peace, democracy and human rights will be mainstreamed.

If such education is to be effective and young people are to recognise its relevance to their lives, it is important that programmes acknowledge the contexts in which they are living and the anti-democratic forces that operate both within communities and across the globe. Education does not take place within a political vacuum. Ministers of Education, meeting at the 1994 UNESCO conference, gave particular priority to the education of children and young people, recognising the potential negative impact of anti-democratic forces on their lives. Not only did they express their conviction that a key aim of education is to promote an active commitment to the defence of human rights and to the building of a culture of peace and democracy, but they prefaced their Declaration by expressing how they were:

> Deeply concerned by the manifestations of violence, racism, xenophobia, aggressive nationalism and violations of human rights, by religious intolerance, by the upsurge of terrorism in all its forms and manifestations and by the growing gap separating wealthy countries from poor countries, phenomena which threaten the consolidation of peace and democracy both nationally and internationally and which are obstacles to development (UNESCO, 1995: 2.2).

Events over the years since the Declaration was passed serve to reinforce such concerns.

The terrorist attacks of 11 September 2001 and their aftermath serve to reinforce the need for an education which prepares young people to live together in an interdependent world. The scale and shock of the attacks left many young people (and adults) feeling vulnerable and powerless. The repercussions are not only felt at national and international levels but also within local communities across the world. For example, in Britain, the USA and in other parts of the world many Muslims, particularly women, and other people judged to be of Middle Eastern or Asian origin or appearance have been subjected to abuse and harassment (Amnesty International, 2001; *The Independent*, 4 January 2002: 30). As one group of US educators reminds us:

> In times of crisis human rights are often called into question, yet if humanity is to advance, these rights and standards must not be set aside, but rather reinforced. Human rights must not be placed on a subordinate plane to political objectives. We must reassert the validity of these rights, and *work to assure that human rights do not become a footnote in the debate over what will and has to be done*. They must form the foundation of not only our personal lives, but also the life of our community and our world. We cannot be selective, not with specific rights nor with specific people, nor with specific countries. Human rights are for ALL people, and by their very nature are indivisible (Amnesty International, 2001, our emphasis).

If we are to ensure that 'human rights do not become a footnote in the debate over what will and has to be done' then we need to ensure that all children are guaranteed their right to education in human rights, in line with the provisions of the UN Convention on the Rights of the Child (Article 29). Such an education must equip children and young people with skills to participate and to effect change, including the skills of language, advocacy and mobilisation. This implies programmes which promote political literacy.

Citizenship and the Challenge of Global Education explores these questions, drawing specifically on our research into the ways in which a number of countries are developing initiatives in this area. We review forms of institutional support for global education in four countries: Denmark, England, the Republic of Ireland and the Netherlands.

In chapter two, we explore alternative narratives of globalisation and consider their impact on international and national education policies. We argue that one of the most critical challenges facing the world community is to influence and shape the processes of globalisation and to support processes of democratisation at all levels, from the local to the global. We explore educational responses to globalisation, examining, first, efforts to create a skilled workforce, capable of competing in a world job market and, secondly, efforts to create cosmopolitan citizens who can participate in democratic processes to resolve the challenges facing the global community. We then reflect on the qualities of a cosmopolitan citizen and on the ways in which teachers might plan a programme of global education. Finally, we examine the implications for schools and communities, addressing the democratisation of schools, the curriculum and the need for lifelong learning. We reflect on how teachers can make sense of the various initiatives designed to bring about a global dimension to the curriculum. In particular we focus on the importance of mainstreaming such initiatives through citizenship education so that learners are equipped with the skills of political literacy and feel that they can make a difference.

Chapters three to six each focuses on a case study of global education within a specific national context. Taking Denmark, England, the Republic of Ireland and the Netherlands in turn, we consider the extent to which government policies encourage an understanding of global interdependence and the development of skills for democratic participation.

We ask how schools are integrating issues of citizenship, human rights and multiculturalism into their curricula, and reflect on the kinds of support they are receiving. We highlight some of the challenges that teachers must face as they seek to interpret education policy within the context of wider social policies.

These chapters draw on an email survey carried out on behalf of the European Commission-funded Thematic Network on Global Education. We developed a questionnaire, which set out to investigate the degree of institutional support for global education in each of the four countries. The questionnaire was circulated to members of the Thematic Network on Global Education and amended in the light of comments received. A copy of the questionnaire is included in an appendix pp.129-130.

In each of the four case study countries we drew up a list of key research respondents, consisting of a range of individuals from a variety of professional contexts. These include ministries, curriculum development agencies, organisations engaged in teacher training at national or local authority levels, non-governmental organisations (NGOs) and special projects. A number of respondents suggested additional or alternative individuals and these were added to our list. Respondents were invited to select from the questions those which they felt competent to address. Additional information was drawn from web pages of various national ministries and NGOs and from earlier research.

The study is particularly concerned with those elements of global education available to learners during the mandatory years of schooling, either at school or in other settings such as youth clubs. We were also interested to establish how global education is supported through initial and in-service teacher training. The initial data collection took place between February and April 2001 and further research took place in autumn 2001 in preparation for this book.

One of the challenges in carrying out the research was to establish a working definition of global education that would be understood by a wide range of respondents, working in a range of professional and cultural contexts across the European Union. For the purposes of the research project we used global education as an umbrella term, explaining that we were concerned in particular with the global dimensions of education for democratic citizenship, development education, environmental education, human rights education, intercultural/multicultural education and peace education. Some aspects may be addressed through established curriculum subjects and others are realised through special initiatives and projects. We provided our respondents with this working definition and referred them to the international definitions drafted by the UNESCO and the North South Centre of the Council of Europe. Respondents were encouraged to use their own terminology, as appropriate.

One clear limitation on the project, imposed by the budget, was the requirement to respond and to provide documentation in English. We do not seek to argue that the four case studies presented are in

7

any way representative of EU States as a whole, in their support for global education. The intention is to provide a snap-shot view of support for global education in each country and to identify similarities and differences of approach which might be of value to policy-makers, officials, teachers, activists and other interested parties. When providing an overview, it is always the case that some generalisations have to be made.

In chapter seven we look at the implications of our findings for policy makers in the British context, and particularly for those in England. It needs to be acknowledged that it is sometimes difficult to make direct comparisons between case study countries. Individual informants in each country have particular interests on which they focused, and these interests may not reflect the full picture. Nevertheless, there are common themes and approaches from which we can learn. In each country initiatives are being taken at all levels, from the classroom, from NGOs and from national ministries to develop international perspectives in the curriculum. Unfortunately, these are not always well co-ordinated, and in some contexts, this 'internationalisation' of education does not appear to extend much beyond Europe. Despite the strong impact of globalisation processes on all our lives, policy-makers, curriculum developers and those developing materials do not always make explicit the connections between local, national, regional and global concerns. There is a frequent tendency to address international issues without considering the, sometimes uncomfortable, parallel concerns in local communities.

We conclude by examining questions of citizenship, identity and belonging in Britain, in order to explore some of the implications of our findings for English schools. We consider the ways in which British citizenship has often been defined by those it has effectively excluded, marginalised or problematised, namely, migrants, those from particular 'visible' minority communities, and people of 'mixed' descent. We demonstrate how, in the face of discrimination and disadvantage, many individuals from African Caribbean and Asian communities in Britain have highlighted new and alternative ways of being citizens. Education for cosmopolitan citizenship, which encourages teachers and learners to make connections between their everyday experiences and those of others in their communities or further afield, provides a means by which global education or education for human rights, democracy and development might be realised. We consider the ways in which cosmopolitan citizens might develop skills of intercultural evaluation, based on human rights principles, which will enable them to live together in culturally diverse communities and in an interdependent world.

2
Globalisation and cosmopolitan citizenship: educational responses

This chapter examines the processes of globalisation and democratisation and considers global education both as a response to these processes and as a way of enabling learners to engage with them and in them. It then explores some of the implications for the education of children and young people.

Since the 1970s, educators have engaged in a number of initiatives designed to enable young people to understand the principles of equality and justice in a context of diversity and change. These include multicultural/intercultural education, development education, and human rights education. We explore the links between these approaches and propose a framework which gives them coherence. Finally, we discuss current attempts to mainstream these concerns within programmes of education for citizenship and reflect on the need to promote political literacy in schools.

Alternative narratives of globalisation
The term globalisation refers to those developments which are increasing levels of global interdependence and which are affecting nearly all aspects of our lives. Dominant narratives of globalisation tend to focus largely or exclusively on economic developments and on the increasing power of transnational companies at the expense of nation states. Yet globalisation is political, technological and cultural as well as economic. It not only relates to the level of world trade and the 'virtual economy' or electronic flow of capital, but also to labour and production, information, ecology, legal and administrative

systems, culture and civil society. Throughout the 1990s there was a debate as to whether globalisation was a meaningful concept, with some asserting that the world economy continues as it has done in the past, and that the world has not changed that much. The focus of the debate has now shifted, and the focus is now on the consequences of globalisation rather than whether or not it exists (Giddens, 2000).

At the same time the 'anti-globalisation' movement has also grown and is exerting pressure. For many people the question is not how to *stop* globalisation, since it is impossible to stop satellite technology, or to ban such things as the spread of popular culture or access to air travel, but how to *influence* and shape it. Those who protested on the streets of Seattle in November 1999 halting the World Trade Organisation (WTO) conference and those who were at Prague the following year were challenging corporate power and inequality. Some, frustrated and disaffected with formal politics, were prepared to use violence. Most significantly, many were organising trans-nationally to express solidarity with the victims of globalisation. Their response is significant in that their efforts mark the beginning of demands for a global response to globalisation. It places the idea of a global civil society on the public agenda.

A number of political theorists argue that we need to re-think demo-cracy in the context of our increasingly interdependent world. Held (1995 and 1996) proposes a model of 'cosmopolitan democracy', challenging the notion that the nation state is the most appropriate locus for democracy. He argues for the building of human rights into the constitution of states and for the creation and development of regional and global institutions, which would coexist alongside states but over-ride them on those issues which escape their control, such as monetary management, environmental questions, elements of security and new forms of communication.

Indeed, many such reforms have been introduced since the mid-1990s. For example, in the UK, the Human Rights Act 1998 incor-porates the European Convention on Human Rights into domestic law. At global and regional levels new mechanisms to promote greater accountability and democracy are also being developed:

> From the UN system to the EU, from changes to the law of war to the entrenchment of human rights, from the emergence of international environmental regimes to the foundation of the International Criminal Court, there is also another narrative being told – the narrative which seeks to reframe human activity and entrench it in law, rights and responsibilities (Held, 2001).

The reforms effectively acknowledge overlapping 'communities of fate' (Held, 1996) and the need for collective democratic solutions, at local, national, regional and global levels.

The terrorist attacks of 11 September 2001 have brought these concerns into sharper focus. Governments and intergovernmental organisations are required to re-think their global responsibilities, and work co-operatively and with moral consistency with regard to human rights, justice and aid. Indeed, it can be argued that for wealthy countries such policies are in their self-interest:

> 11 September decisively shrunk the distance between the world that benefits from globalisation and the world that has been left behind. September 11 also collapsed the justification for keeping national interests safe from infestation by talk of values. Our values tell us to reach out and share the extraordinary bounty of a globalised world with those who have less than we do. Our interests now also tell us that if we don't, we will face an unending struggle in which victory will be forever beyond our grasp (Ignatieff, 2001).

11 September 2001 has caused many groups and organisations to re-think their strategies in reshaping globalisation. Those meeting at the Social Forum in Porto Alegre, Brazil, in 2002, avoided establishing a common programme. Nevertheless, Maude Barlow, director of *Conseil des Canadiens*, one of the organisations represented at the Forum, argued that the Forum was a turning point, as mere opposition to globalisation following 11 September is now inadequate (*Le Monde*, 27/28 January, 2002). It follows that those in solidarity with the victims of globalisation need to engage with its processes and shape them. Consequently at Porto Alegre the issues debated included:

• taxes on the international flow of capital

• abolition of tax havens

- cancellation of third world debt

- re-aligning the balance of power between global economic institutions (World Bank, IMF) and those concerned with protecting human rights (International Labour Organisation, World Health Organisation)

- re-organisation of agricultural policies in favour of smaller producers

- re-invigorating democratic institutions.

There is a growing awareness that the dream of a globalised free market is a misguided, ideologically driven, utopian, non-sustainable social experiment that could have catastrophic consequences:

> The west greeted the collapse of communism – though it was itself a western utopian ideology – as the triumph of western values. The end of the most catastrophic utopian experiment in history was welcomed as a historic opportunity to launch another vast utopian project – a global free market. The world was to be made over in an image of western modernity (Gray, 2001).

A wide range of organisations is now engaged in influencing the future shape of globalisation. Amongst the 10,000 official delegates at the Social Forum were representatives of international humanitarian and development organisations such as *Médecins sans frontières* and Oxfam; environmental groups such as Greenpeace and Friends of the Earth; trade unions; and alliances against Third World Debt (see figure 2.1). They are challenging the policies of the World Bank, the International Monetary Fund and the World Trade Organisation. Some are committed to various forms of direct action. For the majority, the intention is to bring about change through democratic participation. In other words, they are seeking to make globalisation itself a more democratic process.

As the presence of community based organisations at the Social Forum testifies, the effects of globalisation are experienced at local levels and these too need to be addressed through new and deeper forms of democracy. One of the most visible expressions of change in Europe is the presence of migrants, refugees and asylum seekers from across the world. Inclusive societies must be predicated on a

Figure 2.1: Re-shaping Globilisation: disparate groups and alliances

(adapted from Le Monde)

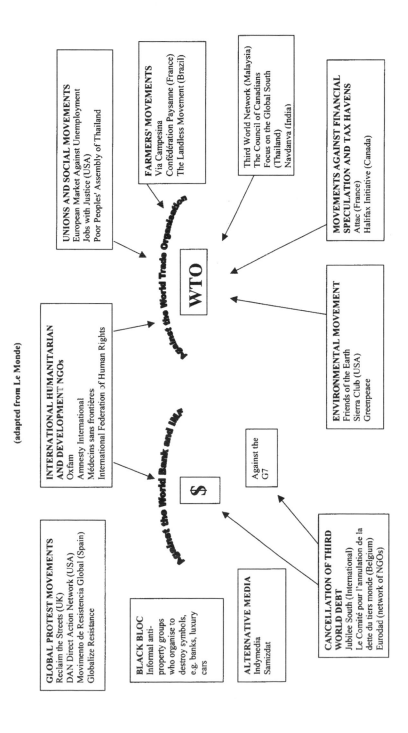

model of democracy which ensures both equality and respect for difference. It is for this reason that antiracism as a key condition for democracy is high on the agenda both in Europe and at a global level (Osler and Starkey, 2002a) as evidenced by the UN World Conference Against Racism held in Durban, in September 2001. Antiracism needs to be recognised as more than the opposite to racism but as a set of values, beliefs and actions which are part of a broader human rights discourse and project.

Beck (2001), in a response to the events of 11 September 2001, stresses that cosmopolitan democracy involves solidarity and respect for difference within communities and states as well as at a global level:

> What are we fighting for when we fight against global terrorism? My answer is that we should fight for the right to be cosmopolitan, which is fundamentally based on the recognition of the otherness of others. ...Cosmopolitan states emphasise the necessity for solidarity with foreigners both inside and outside the national borders...[they] struggle not only against terror, but against the causes of terror. ...they do this by seeking the solution of global problems... which cannot be solved by individual nations on their own (Beck, 2001).

This requires us to re-examine how the concept of identity can enable social and political solidarity. Gilroy (2000) examines two ways in which a shared identity can be imagined to support the development of cosmopolitan democracy. First, he draws on the example of South Africa and on President Nelson Mandela's efforts to create a new democratic consciousness, national solidarity and cohesion by appealing to a common relationship to the land. In his inaugural speech as State President, Mandela appealed to a shared connection with and stewardship of the land, in order to build a sense of shared citizenship, solidarity and oneness. In doing so he challenged the violence of apartheid as a violation of South Africa's natural beauty and of nature itself:

> To my compatriots, I have no hesitation in saying that each one of us is as intimately attached to the soil of this beautiful country as are the famous jacaranda trees of Pretoria and the mimosa trees of the bushveld.

> Each time one of us touches the soil of this land, we feel a sense of personal renewal ... That spiritual and physical onesness we all share with this common homeland explains the depth of pain we all carried in our hearts as we saw our country tear itself apart in a terrible conflict (Nelson Mandela, May, 1995, quoted in Gilroy, 2000: 111).

The appeal is to a new South African national identity based on a 'common homeland' and on shared humanity in order to realise common citizenship and cosmopolitan democracy. Under apartheid some communities drew on their histories to develop mutually exclusive identities and others had seen their communities shatter as they were forcibly moved from them. At this particular point in South Africa's development it appeared impossible to appeal to a common shared history. Mandela uses the land as a means of enabling diverse groups to feel a common sense of belonging. Nevertheless, the notion of a common homeland has considerable limitations. When it is used to establish a link between the land and one exclusive identity this has led to ethnic conflicts and wars.

In post-colonial societies, many people may have difficulties in identifying with the nation state. Gilroy proposes an alternative way of creating a shared identity, which does not rely on territory, but which is placeless. He draws on the example of the African Diaspora and the difficulties, identified by Martin Luther King, of black Americans in the 1960s whose loyalty to their country was undermined by their lack of economic and political rights. Identity is established through a shared history which promotes solidarity and action, although 'the role of victim has its drawbacks as the basis of any political identity' (Gilroy, 2000: 113) and may hinder the development of alliances based on a broader shared commitment to address inequality and injustice. Solidarity is not confined to those who have experienced the suffering, or their descendants, but is a matter of justice. It is therefore the responsibility of all, including the majority who are unlikely to recognise themselves as having a direct link with either the perpetrators or victims:

> to possess those histories and consider setting them to work in divining more modest and more plausible understandings of democracy, tolerance for difference, and cross-cultural recognition (Gilroy, 2000: 114).

It is by acknowledging the past, understanding injustice and recognising that the history of Europe and of the nation state has not been a steady march of progress that we can recognise and avoid the danger of constructing mutually impermeable national identities. Such mutually impermeable national identities have regularly led to conflict, violence and war as, for example, in Northern Ireland and Bosnia-Herzegovina. The need is for solidarity 'inside and outside national borders'. Indeed, there are a number of preconditions that need to be fulfilled if the democratisation of transnational institutions and organisations is to be effective and if these organisations are to be accountable. It is important that individuals and groups:

- recognise our common humanity and interdependence

- have a sense of belonging to a global community

- organise to express solidarity with the victims of globalisation

- exercise rights to participation from the local through to the global levels.

These processes of democratisation at a global level require a new vision of education for cosmopolitan citizenship.

Educational responses to globalisation

In the UK, a key Government response to the processes of globalisation is the determination to raise standards of achievement in education, so that learners will have the skills to compete successfully in a world job market. The emphasis is on the basic skills of literacy and numeracy:

> A generation ago Britain tolerated an education system with a long tail of poor achievement because there was a plentiful supply of unskilled and semi-skilled jobs. This is no longer the case. By breaking the cycle of underachievement in education we can extend opportunity across society.

> To prosper in the 21st century competitive global economy, Britain must transform the knowledge and skills of its population. Every child, whatever their circumstances, requires an education that equips them for work and prepares them to succeed in the wider economy and in society (DfES, 2001: 5. 1.1 and 1.2).

The 2001 Government White Paper on Education, *Schools Achieving Success*, stresses accountability, inspection, meeting the needs of the individual, consumer choice and improved incentives for teacher performance as means by which educational standards can be raised in this global competition. The White Paper emphasises diversity, but this is diversity in the provision of schools, so that they can cater for the 'diverse requirements and aspirations' of learners, 'particularly beyond the age of 14, when the talents of pupils diversify' (*Ibid*: 6). The aim is to provide either academic or vocational opportunities for these diverse learners, since it is believed that the existing, predominantly academic, curriculum is failing many of them. Research evidence indicates a long history of young people from particular minority ethnic groups being channelled into lower ability streams and lower status vocational qualifications (Eggleston *et al.*, 1986; Osler, 1997a; Gillborn and Youdell, 2000). Despite this evidence, the proposed arrangements do not include monitoring of academic and vocational 'options' to ensure equal access for all.

There is no reference in the White Paper to cultural diversity, nor to the community learning and experiences of citizenship which young people bring to school (Osler and Starkey, 2001a and 2002b, forthcoming). There is, however, passing reference to 'substantial variations in standards between different parts of the country, between girls and boys, and between different social and ethnic groups' (DfES, 2001: 10. 2.13). Young people are expected to learn 'how to reason, think logically and creatively and take increasing responsibility for their own learning' (*Ibid.*, 18. 3.2). This would seem to imply processes of democratisation in schools, but legislative proposals do not address student participation or representation in school decision-making. Instead, they focus on deregulation of schools, 'failing' schools and local authorities, and performance-related pay. The accountability of schools and education authorities does not appear to extend to learners who, though responsible for their own learning, are not guaranteed involvement in school governance or in decision-making relating to the curriculum. There is no legislation to ensure that young people are consulted about matters or procedures affecting them, in line with Article 12 of the UN Convention on the Rights of the Child. Nor are there any processes for student appeal if an individual believes they have experienced an injustice.

For some years now, one response to the forces of globalisation has been for governments to place greater emphasis on the need for education systems to respond to the need for international competitiveness, rather than to emphasise the need for greater international understanding. The pressure on schools is therefore to improve standards so that students will be well placed to make their contribution to an internationally competitive workforce. Globalisation is seen largely as an economic process and not as a potential force for greater democratisation. The White Paper is a response to economic globalisation but it ignores the need for greater democratisation as a means of shaping and influencing the ongoing processes of globalisation. Yet without political leadership, education for peace, human rights and democracy is unlikely to be widely recognised as a mainstream issue. It is unlikely to be addressed as a priority in the day-to-day management of schools or to feature on the agenda of headteachers' management training.

Beck (2000) observes that in Germany there is also recognition of the need to develop an education policy response to economic globalisation. This is seen in terms of developing a learning society, with an emphasis on flexibility and lifelong learning. He identifies some of the other skills required to enable citizens to live together in an increasingly interdependent world:

> One of the main political responses to globalisation is therefore *to build and develop the education and knowledge society*; to make training longer rather than shorter; to loosen or do away with its link to a particular job or occupation, gearing it instead to key qualifications that can be widely used in practice. This should not only be understood in terms of 'flexibility' or 'lifelong learning', but should also cover such things as social competence, the ability to work in a team, conflict resolution, understanding of other cultures, integrated thinking, and a capacity to handle uncertainties, and paradoxes' (Beck, 2000: 137-138).

These social skills, together with basic skills of literacy and numeracy, are, of course, essential for participation in the workforce as well as for cosmopolitan citizenship. If citizens are to shape the processes of globalisation and participate in democratic processes at local, national and regional levels, schools will need to prepare learners for global as well as national citizenship. The processes of globalisation and democratisation demand education for peace, democracy and human rights and the development of a global ethic. As one UK Government education policy adviser has expressed it:

> If we want young people to learn the rules of living and working in communities – how to solve differences of opinion, how to respect a variety of beliefs, how to make collective decisions in a democratic society, and so on – then these must feature in the curriculum of schools.

> ...School leaders will need to see themselves increasingly as citizens of the world. If that sounds implausible, unrealistic or naïve it is worth noting that in the world financial markets and many areas of business it has already occurred. If the global marketplace is to operate within a framework of morality based on notions of a democratic society and focused on solving the huge range of global challenges ahead, then the time left for schools and their leaders to catch up is limited (Barber, 1996: 187-8, 237-8).

UNESCO reminds us of the social and political context, which makes global education so critical:

> a period of transition and accelerated change marked by the expression of intolerance, manifestations of racial and ethnic hatred, the upsurge of terrorism in all its forms and manifestations, discrimination, war and violence towards those regarded as 'other' and the growing disparities between rich and poor, at international and national levels alike (UNESCO, 1995).

Global education
Since global education implies education for sustainable development, it needs to address sustainability at both local and global levels. For communities to be sustainable, it is critical that education addresses political sustainability as well as environmental, social and economic sustainability. This implies an education rooted in democratic practice, where learners recognise that their own world-view and many of their values are not universally shared; understand

the complexity of differences and similarities; and develop the social and political skills to become effective participants in decision-making, who are able to resolve conflicts peacefully.

An educated cosmopolitan citizen will be confident in his or her own identities and will work to achieve peace, human rights and democracy within the local community and at a global level, by:

- developing skills to cope with change and uncertainty

- accepting personal responsibility and recognising the importance of civic commitment

- working collaboratively to solve problems and achieve a just, peaceful and democratic community

- respecting diversity between people, according to gender, ethnicity and culture

- recognising that their own worldview is shaped by personal and societal history and by cultural tradition

- recognising that no individual or group holds the only answer to problems

- understanding that there may be a range of solutions to problems

- respecting and negotiating with others on the basis of equality

- showing solidarity with and compassion for others

- resolving conflict in a non-violent way

- making informed choices and judgements

- having a vision of a preferred future

- respecting the cultural heritage

- protecting the environment

- adopting methods of production and consumption which lead to sustainable development

- working to achieve harmony between immediate basic needs and long-term interests

- promoting solidarity and equity at national and international levels (adapted from UNESCO *Declaration and Integrated Framework of Action on Education for Peace, Human Rights and Democracy*, 1995).

One useful way in which teachers might identify and organise the subject matter of global education was proposed by the World Studies Project in the publication *Learning for Change in World Society* (Richardson, 1979) (see Figure 2.2). Drawing on this framework, we pose four key questions relating to the challenges facing the global community; the background of those challenges, including their historical causes; the action that might be taken; and the values that underpin a just community and a just world.

Figure 2.2 (Adapted from Richardson, 1979)

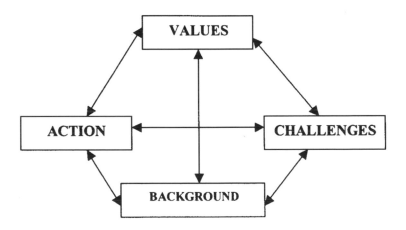

What **challenges** face the global community? What are the issues that need to be resolved which require co-operation at a global level, at regional and national levels and within local communities? The global problems identified by UNESCO are intolerance, racism, terrorism, discrimination, violence and war, and poverty. Many are also problems for local communities. The goal is to achieve human rights, sustainable development and peace.

What is the **background** to these issues and problems? How can we better understand these developments and their impact on individuals and communities? What do we need to know about the history of these issues; the environments in which they occur; the actions and attitudes of individuals, groups and governments; the social, political and economic institutions? How do these different factors relate to each other?

What **action** might be taken and what action is being taken? What needs to be done in the long term to tackle the underlying causes and improve things? What can and is being done now to tackle the worst effects? What can be done by international organisations, by governments, by groups and by individuals?

What sort of a world do we want to move towards? What **values** are important? What sort of world order do we want? What kinds of organisation would allow for greater participation and democracy at global, regional, national and local levels?

Figure 2.2 reminds us that in taking action there are three key goals: to face directly the challenge of the immediate problem; to tackle the long-term background to the problem we are seeking to resolve; and to realise particular values. Similarly, values have three separate aspects: values affect how people see the problem in the first place, they help shape the worldview of the individual, which in turn is shaped by their personal and societal history and cultural tradition. Values will affect how we analyse the underlying causes (background) and how (or whether) we engage in action for change. Similarly, the challenges facing the individual and the global community and the ways in which they have been identified are influenced by the values of individuals and communities; by history and by current political, social and economic structures; and by past and present actions. The analysis requires an approach which takes account of historical factors but which is also orientated towards the future and towards change.

In analysing global education in this way we are required to focus on two further concerns. They relate to values, judgements and action in contexts of cultural pluralism. First, how can we engage in collective decision-making and action in schools or other multicultural learning communities? How should we make judgements, without imposing our own worldview on others? Secondly, can a system of shared values be established in a multicultural or plural context?

Figueroa reminds us that 'all present-day societies (if not, indeed, all societies) are plural' (2000: 52). Pluralism does not imply that all people necessarily have equal status or power within a society, but it does assume that, as human beings, they are of equal worth. While we may assume that any culture has some basic worth and is deserving of respect, this does not imply that we should accept every aspect of another person's culture, simply because it is their culture. In any case no culture is fixed or homogeneous. All cultures are dynamic and encompass diversity. Judgements are inevitable, even if they are also provisional and subject to revision or correction. As Figueroa expresses it:

> Pluralism does not mean a radical relativism. That would be self-defeating. One must stand somewhere. It is not possible to stand nowhere.
>
> ... Of course there can be conflicts. ... Ultimately, differences and problems must be resolved by discourse – if they are not to be dealt with by violence. The process must be constant and constantly re-newed (Figueroa, 2000: 55 and 56).

This implies that we acquire skills of intercultural communication. However, it implies more than this. Since 'one must stand some-where' and have a critical respect for other cultures it is important that individuals acquire skills of intercultural evaluation (Hall, 2000; Parekh, 2000b). Internationally agreed human rights texts provide us with a set of principles against which we can assess our own and others' cultures and reflect on our values. Human rights imply reciprocity, that is a duty or responsibility to respect and protect the rights of others:

> An absolutist and sovereignly individualistic human rights discourse can be counter-productive, leading to conflict by neglecting responsibilities and mutuality. Human rights are the rights of concrete individuals-with-others (Figueroa, 2000: 52).

Human rights can also provide the framework for the development of a set of shared values in a community such as a school. This does not imply that all the values held by individuals will be agreed but

25

that a diverse community, drawing its values from a range of cultures, religious and secular traditions, will be able to derive a set of core values based on universally agreed human rights principles.

The realisation of global education will require attention being given to democratic processes, institutional ethos and community as well as to the curriculum. The next section explores each of these in turn, ending with the relationship between global education and lifelong learning.

Democratising schools

As we have suggested in the introduction, for global education to be effective 'the atmosphere of the institution must be in harmony with the application of democratic standards' (UNESCO: 1995: IV. 17). In other words, global education, which is a response to the need for greater democratisation at all levels from the local to the global, needs to include a commitment to democracy within the learning institution. This implies that schools need to address questions relating to climate and ethos and be committed to a process of democratisation. An individual teacher committed to developing global perspectives in the curriculum may be able to realise this within her own classroom. It is unlikely, however, that any young person will acquire all the attributes of cosmopolitan citizenship detailed above without the opportunity to practice them with the school community and wider society.

Figure 2.3 is a model of a democratic school, based on human rights principles. It was developed out of an action research project developed by an individual teacher, in which she set out to enable a group of boys to develop the skills necessary to resolve conflicts in a non-violent way, by introducing a programme based on human rights principles (Carter, 2000; Carter and Osler, 2000). The research suggests that realisation of children's human rights in school requires a fundamental change in school culture. In particular, there is a need to review the basis of relationships between teachers and learners and to develop forms of school discipline in co-operation with learners (Osler, 2000b). The process of school democratisation requires that teachers, as well as students, are given real opportunities to participate in school decision-making. This

Figure 2.3: Democratising the School (adapted from Carter and Osler, 2000)

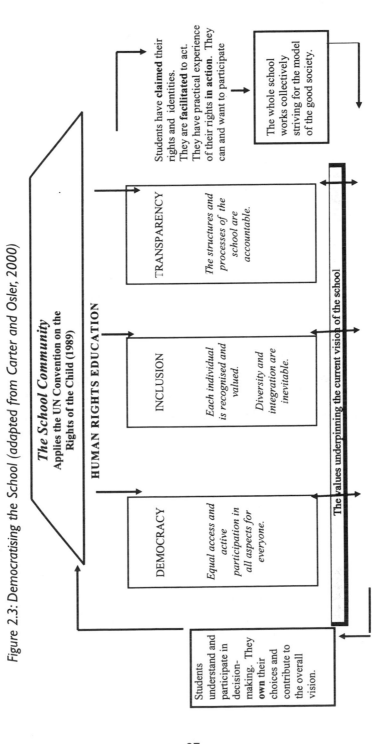

The School Community
Applies the UN Convention on the Rights of the Child (1989)

HUMAN RIGHTS EDUCATION

Students have **claimed** their rights and identities.
They are **facilitated** to act.
They have practical experience of their rights **in action**. They can and want to participate

The whole school works collectively striving for the model of the good society.

TRANSPARENCY

The structures and processes of the school are accountable.

INCLUSION

Each individual is recognised and valued.

Diversity and integration are inevitable.

DEMOCRACY

Equal access and active participation in all aspects for everyone.

The values underpinning the current vision of the school

Students understand and participate in decision-making. They **own** their choices and contribute to the overall vision.

27

implies a progressive introduction of democratic methods so that staff and students have time to work with them in an atmosphere of relative security.

The model proposes three 'pillars' for a school where children's rights are protected: democracy, inclusion and transparency. Democratic structures alone are unlikely to be sufficient. In contexts of diversity, they need to be matched by a commitment to and means of insuring the inclusion of all. This implies structures which support and monitor the participation of potentially marginalised groups of students. So, for example, it will be insufficient simply to establish a student council. Consideration will also have to be given to mechanisms which guarantee the participation of diverse groups of young people in the decision-making body. The participation of both girls and boys may be achieved readily by ensuring that each class elects one female and one male representative, but further efforts will be required to guarantee the participation of young people with special educational needs and those from a full range of social, ethnic and cultural backgrounds.

In the process of democratisation, the school will need to develop means of self-evaluation (Osler and Starkey, 1998 and 2001b). It is through such means that organisational processes become transparent and schools are accountable to their members. Effective grievance and complaints procedures are an important element in an institution which seeks to guarantee the rights of learners and which aims to support them in taking responsibility for their learning. The existence of such procedures will contribute to an atmosphere where young people feel they have a voice and these procedures are also likely to support a disciplined learning environment.

School and community
If a central goal of global education is to enable the development of cosmopolitan citizens equipped to play an active part in shaping future local and global communities then the school needs to recognise the ways in which students are currently developing citizenship skills within their local communities. Students will also need opportunities to put into practice the learning that takes place in school, thus making a contribution to the development of just, peaceful and

democratic communities. This implies that the school is a part of the community in which it is situated and that parents and other community members have an opportunity to play a role in the development of the school. Many schools in England are disadvantaged in their efforts to establish effective partnerships with parents and communities because the make-up of the teaching staff does not reflect that of the local community. Acting as a school governor is one means by which individuals can practice citizenship. Schools with governing bodies that reflect the social and cultural diversity of the local community are more likely to be key agencies within the community:

> A culturally diverse governing body helps to ensure the effective flow of information between the school and the community it serves. Diverse representation also sends out the message that the school is taking steps to address the educational interests of all the stakeholders in the community. Additionally, diversity in the composition of the governing body often links the governing body to other influential groups in the community. ...a governing body that reflects the interests in the locality is likely to develop school policies that are relevant to pupils from all cultural groups (Gittens, 2000: 181-182).

Curriculum

Since the 1970s, teachers have pursued a number of projects designed to enable young people to understand the principles of equality, justice, co-operation, non-violence, tolerance and respect for cultural diversity. These include multicultural/intercultural education, development education, peace education and human rights education.

A number of writers have traced the development of multicultural education in England, recognising the key role which local communities and also particular local education authorities (LEAs) have played in the development of multicultural and anti-racist initiatives (for example, Klein, 1992; Osler, 1997a). Although certain local education authorities have played a key role, the UK government has never actively promoted a curriculum which set out to promote race equality; when a national curriculum for England was introduced in the 1990s, an attempt to introduce a multicultural dimension was quietly dropped (Tomlinson, 1993). In other countries, such as Canada, multiculturalism has been promoted as a state policy and education has played a key role in the development of multicultural policies. In the UK, the implementation of the Race Relations (Amendment) Act 2000 marks a significant change of emphasis. Under this legislation, schools and other public bodies are required not merely to avoid discrimination but to promote race equality. Inspection agencies, including OFSTED, will be required to monitor how they are doing so (Osler, 2002).

By contrast, initiatives to promote development education have been supported, not by local communities but by the international aid NGOs, concerned that there should be public awareness of issues relating to development and interdependence. In the UK, development education began to receive government funding in 1997, following the election of a Labour government. Human rights education, promoted by such bodies as UNESCO and the Council of Europe, grew in importance during the 1980s, but it was not until the 1990s that it was widely recognised that development education and human rights education are inextricably linked (Starkey, 1994).

Each of these traditions has been developed by schools to varying degrees, depending on the sources of local support available. The challenge is recognise that each is linked one to the other, since the local, regional and global problems we face are also linked. So, for example, so-called ethnic conflicts are often about access to resources, or the unequal allocation of scarce resources in a region. Parents petitioning local authorities to introduce traffic calming measures may be thinking, first and foremost, about the safety of their children, but the introduction of such measures on a wider scale would go some way towards addressing the problem of carbon monoxide levels, which in turn might have an impact on global warming. Children learning about the UN Convention on the Rights of the Child, and children's rights across the globe, will be able to make links between these rights and school policies to tackle bullying. In developing a coherent approach to global education, teachers need to be able to make the links between such issues and enable their students to do likewise.

Lifelong learning

UNESCO has emphasised the lifelong nature of global education, stressing that it should be available to adults as well as young people, should address vulnerable groups, and take place in informal as well as formal settings:

> It is equally urgent to organise special youth programmes, laying emphasis on participation by children and young people in solidarity actions and environmental protection.
>
> The education of citizens cannot be the exclusive responsibility of the education sector. If it is to be able to do its job effectively in this field, the education sector should closely co-operate, in particular, with the family, the media, including traditional channels of communication, the world of work and NGOs.
>
> Young people who spend a lot of time outside school and who often do not have access to the formal education system, or to vocational training or a job, as well as young people doing their military service, are a very important target group of education programmes for peace, human rights and democracy. ...it is therefore essential for them to be able to receive non-formal education adapted to their needs, which would prepare them to assume their role as citizens in a responsible and effective way (UNESCO, 1995: 27, 32, 34 and 35).

If global education for cosmopolitan citizenship is to be effective, it must extend beyond the school into the youth sector and parents and families must be engaged in the project. The media needs to be a partner in this education, and young people and adults need to acquire the skills to critically interpret what they see and read.

Mainstreaming global education

A number of commentators have observed the increasing importance which citizenship education is being given in a range of countries world-wide. In a section entitled 'Rethinking Civic Education', the co-ordinators of the IEA study on *Citizenship and Education in Twenty-Eight Countries* observe:

> New global realities call for a major reconsideration by educators and policy makers of how young people are being prepared to participate in democratic societies in the early 21st century (Torney-Purta et al., 2001).

31

Similarly, UNESCO has recommended that:

> civics education, whose value was increasingly apparent in many countries, be strengthened in school curricula, especially in multi-ethnic societies, in order to promote harmony and social bonding (UNESCO, 2000: 3 viii).

We argue that while curriculum planners and educators need to identify opportunities for global education across all subjects, citizenship education provides a vehicle through which global education can be mainstreamed. In other words, while it is important that global education permeates the whole curriculum, strategically it also needs a focus within a specific area of the curriculum so that it has a clear status and resources can be appropriately targeted.

We have argued that global education, or education for cosmopolitan citizenship, must of necessity address peace, human rights, democracy and development. It must be orientated towards the future, preparing young citizens to play an active role in shaping the world, at all levels, from the local to the global. The forces of globalisation make this a pressing task. This is about equipping young people with the knowledge, skills and attitudes to enable them to make a difference.

Young people want to make a difference. They want a more peaceful world, where racism, religious intolerance and inequality are challenged. Our research in Leicester, with young people aged 10-18 years, which set out to explore their understandings of community, identity and citizenship, revealed their sensitivity to injustice, poverty and suffering in other parts of the world. Many of them had been involved in campaigns or political action to address issues in their local communities (such as the closure of a school), but faced with injustice or suffering in more distant places, the most common response was to donate money to charity. Fund-raising was supported and promoted by schools (Osler and Starkey, 2001a and 2002b forthcoming). Students were not equipped to explore the political dimensions of the issues which concerned them.

Developing the skills of political literacy is an essential aspect of global education. We have argued that education for a sustainable

32

future requires an understanding not only of environmental, social and economic aspects of sustainability but also of political aspects. Political literacy requires knowledge and understanding of how political systems work, as well as skills to participate and effect change: for example, skills of language, advocacy and mobilisation. In our increasingly interdependent world it is vital that cosmopolitan citizens are equipped to tackle challenges at all levels, including the global.

promote mutual understanding and successful co-existence between majority and minority populations, such as anti-discrimination laws. In comparison with other EU countries, there is minimal support in Denmark for the 'repatriation' of migrants. There is however some cause for concern: Denmark is a polarised country. It has a large percentage of intolerant people (20 per cent) as well as the highest percentage of actively tolerant (33 per cent, on a par with Sweden) in the EU. Nearly one third (32 per cent) of Danes expressed negative feelings towards people of other religions, stating that they find the presence of people of another religion disturbing (Thalhammer, *et al.*, 2001).

There is fear of social conflict and a possible decline in welfare benefits as a result of immigration. Additionally, there is an exceptionally widespread concern that educational standards will decline if the percentage of children from minority groups in school is too high. More than three-quarters of respondents (78 per cent) fear a decline in educational standards, the highest percentage of any EU country. Yet 63 per cent of Danes also felt that, where schools make the necessary efforts, the education of all children can be enriched by the presence of children from minority groups (*Ibid.*). There remains considerable ambivalence. Ambivalent people may well respond positively to effective political and educational leadership. Without such leadership, there is a danger that far-right, anti-democratic political parties may exploit fears and concerns,

Denmark provides a clear example of the way in which a change of government can have an immediate impact on policies related to migrants and education. Following the general election in November 2001 the new Government, a coalition between *Venstre* (the liberal party) and *Konservative* (the conservative party), abolished local government obligations to offer immigrants mother-tongue teaching:

> The government wish (sic) to abolish the municipalities' obligation to offer immigrants mother tongue teaching as the government believes successful integration depends on mastering of the Danish language (Danish Ministry of Education, 2001).

Democratic schooling

In Denmark, schooling is compulsory between the ages of 6 and 16. There is no division into primary and secondary schooling, and students progress from year to year through the *folkeskole*, usually with the same cohort and same teachers. There is virtually no streaming, with most classes comprising a heterogeneous group.

Danish education has always been decentralised. The *folkeskole* is financed by the state through a block grant that is given to the municipalities. The Government sets broad parameters but within these, municipalities have considerable freedom within which to implement the general guidance they receive. There is a broad national curriculum structure but within that there is wide scope for variety based on local government decisions and it is much less prescriptive than the UK national curriculum. Decisions on the exact content of the curriculum are taken at the local level (Eurydice, 2000a).

An even greater degree of decentralisation occurred after the *Folkeskole* Act 1989, which resulted in more decision-making power being delegated from the Ministry of Education to the municipalities and from the municipalities to local schools. School boards, on which parents have high representation, now have greater powers than in the past. More recently the law has been further revised. The school is required to model democracy and teachers are advised not to restrict student decision-making to a timetabled class meeting but to use every possible opportunity to promote student participation in decision-making (Hahn, 1999).

In Denmark, classroom teachers have a much greater pastoral care role than teachers in the other case study countries and there is considerable focus on participatory democracy and lessons in citizenship. Students, for example, are encouraged to make decisions jointly with teachers about the direction of lessons, discuss and resolve class problems and disciplinary issues, and plan class visits. From Year 7 onwards, they select the topics they wish to investigate in their social studies class, which covers politics, economics, sociology and international relations. Collaboration, consensus and education for citizenship and democracy are viewed by Danish students as being as important as the achievement of academic goals (Osborn, 1999).

37

Hahn (1999) notes how students are able to develop their decision-making skills within a familiar, supportive community and that the topics they study are ones in which they have a genuine interest and concern. She recalls how in 1995 she observed a Year 9 class who had decided to study the war in former Yugoslavia, the break up of the Soviet Union, and racism in Europe. Previous topics they had undertaken included the Gulf War, the Danish referendum on the Maastricht Treaty and the US presidential election. This broad coverage of current affairs and contemporary politics had been selected as a result of in-depth discussion, in which students had considered a range of alternatives. Consequently, there was genuine interest in the topics under consideration.

Kragh (1996) argues that this kind of environment, where children are encouraged to develop their decision-making skills, also contributes to their psychological development, enabling them to become 'active optimists' (Oscarsson, 1996), that is, citizens who feel positive about their chances of influencing the world in which they live. The IEA comparative study of citizenship education in 28 countries found that 91 per cent of Danish 14-year-olds surveyed in 1999 intended to vote in national elections as an adult. This was among the highest proportions recorded, and compares with just 80 per cent of young people in England and 85 per cent in the United States. Just 51 per cent of young Danes expected to collect money for a social cause or charity; this compares with 59 per cent for the international sample (Torney-Purta *et al.*, 2001).

Non-compulsory national examinations are available at upper secondary level or *gymnasium*, which 50 per cent of students attend for three-year post 16 courses. Alternative two-year programmes are available for other students. In total, 94 per cent of Danish students attend some form of post-compulsory upper secondary provision. Students choose whether or not to sit examinations in consultation with their parents and teacher. Examination results are not published and there is no system of external inspection. At this level, as in the *folkeskole*, students select topics they will study in the majority of their courses. Social studies can be taken as a specialised option at this level but all students continue with some lessons in this field and in politics. For many students such classes involve an in-depth project and group work. Students are required to engage in research, drawing on a range of sources, including libraries and surveys. They must identify a key research question or problem, to introduce the subject, present alternative points of view and then present and justify their own position. The assessment procedures require that students develop these skills of co-operative group work and analysis (Hahn, 1999).

In Denmark there is a much less hierarchical structure to the teaching profession than in the UK and teachers are generally given a greater degree of autonomy in relation to teaching methods and selection of curriculum materials. There is also an expectation among parents of inclusivity in educational decision-making and closer collaborative relationships than are evident in the UK (Mahony, 1998). The commitment to democracy in schools is to be found in school structures as well as in the classroom, with municipalities allocating funds to school boards, consisting of parent, staff and student representatives, which then allocate money to student councils (Hahn, 1999). Thus student democracy is institutionalised and funded within the Danish system. The school system reflects the wider democratic culture:

> The many opportunities that Danish students have for democratic participation occurs in a wider cultural context in which their parents participate in decision-making bodies at work and in which national referenda are commonplace (Hahn, 1999: 235).

The composition of school boards consists of 5 to 7 parent representatives, 2 teacher representatives and two student representatives 'elected by and from the pupils of the school' (Danish Ministry of Education, 1997). Thus, parents have a very powerful voice in the running of schools and the legal framework also ensures the participation of students. Danish parents also have a voice in education decision-making through *Skole og Samfund* (School and Society), a national organisation which aims to strengthen the *folkeskole* and provides training for school board members and a regular magazine for parents. *Skole og Samfund* is a member of the European Parents' Association (EPA) (Skole og Samfund, 2002).

The Act on Democracy in the Education System 2000 means that students will be able to exert yet more direct influence on their day-to-day school life. It gives them the right to set up student councils and confirms their right to have representatives on the school board (equivalent to school governors) as well as any other committee set up by the school that deals with issues of interest to students. It applies to both the *folkeskole* and upper secondary school.

Ministry of Education initiatives

Global education is not a term that is widely used in Denmark. Rather, the Ministry of Education refers to 'the international dimension' in its official documents. Immigrant and refugee populations mean that classrooms now contain a greater number and range of cultures and more emphasis is put on 'intercultural competence' (Muller and Timm, 2001).

One of the three general objectives in the *Folkeskole* Act 1993 draws attention to the importance of the 'international dimension', the environment and social justice:

> The Folkeskole shall familiarise the pupils with Danish culture and contribute to their understanding of other cultures and of human interactions with nature. The school shall prepare the pupils for active participation, joint responsibility, rights and duties in a society based on freedom and democracy. The teaching of the school and its daily life must therefore build on intellectual freedom, equality and democracy (Danish Ministry of Education, 1995, Section 1).

In order to support this objective the Danish Ministry of Education has recently published a booklet, *The International Dimension in the Subjects and Themes of the Folkeskole* (1998). This booklet suggests how global education can be promoted within various subject areas. It emphasises the importance of educating Danish citizens to have comprehensive insights and understandings about global interdependence in relation to economics, the environment, and culture, and in relation to social responsibility and justice.

Several Danish educators in our study emphasised that this publication makes recommendations rather than provides official guidance. They suggested that while there is widespread agreement on the importance of the international dimension within the curriculum, legislative support in the form of direct and explicit policy guidelines and official documents remains limited. One respondent argued that this lack of explicit direction concerning what is meant by the 'international dimension' and how it might best be implemented means that, in practice, the incorporation of a global perspective is largely dependent on the efforts of some enthusiastic teachers and some non-governmental organisations (NGOs). It is perhaps worth setting this statement in the context of our other case studies. Given that many Danish students and teachers already select international issues and topics for study, it may be that this educator merely has higher expectations than educators in other contexts of the degree to which the curriculum should be internationalised.

In July 2000 the Ministry of Education amalgamated three smaller organisations and set up Cirius (the Centre for International Co-operation and Mobility in Education and Training), an independent institution within the Ministry of Education. This centre serves as a national knowledge base and is responsible for strengthening the internationalisation of education and training in Denmark and for managing all the EU programmes involving education, youth and vocational training. Cirius acts as the national agency for the three large EC education programmes, Leonardo, Socrates and Youth for Europe, as well as for other programmes and initiatives (www. ciriusonline.dk/eng).

Other Ministry initiatives

The Ministry of Foreign Affairs was identified by respondents as the other main source of government support for global education initiatives, although the Ministry of Labour was also noted as supporting some global education initiatives in relation to labour market training centres.

Danida is the organisation responsible for development aid from the Danish state and comes under the direction of the Ministry of Foreign Affairs. It has an information fund to which organisations and individuals can apply twice a year. The funding (€3.5 million per annum, at the time of writing) goes towards projects, materials and meetings aimed at raising public awareness about global issues. The formal education sector is seen as an important ally and receives considerable support from Danida. Many of the materials and projects relating to global education originate from this fund. However, the limited co-operation between the Ministry of Education and the Ministry of Foreign Affairs is a point of some frustration for some NGOs (Muller and Timm, 2001).

Human Rights Education

The Danish Centre for Human Rights was established by a parliamentary decision in May 1987. The main aim of the Centre is to gather and develop knowledge about human rights nationally and internationally. The work of the Centre includes research, information, education, and documentation relating to Danish, European and international human rights conditions. In its work, the Centre collaborates with other national, European and international human rights and humanitarian organisations.

The *Youth for Human Rights* project was initiated by the Danish Centre for Human Rights in collaboration with the Danish Youth Council to commemorate the 50th anniversary of the European Convention on Human Rights. It involved inviting European youth to participate in the creation of a Youth Plan of Action. From March to October 2001 an on-line debate and conference on human rights and democracy in Europe took place, to which youth organisations in Europe were invited to send contributions towards a Youth Plan of Action. In 2002, in the second stage of this project, a face-to-face conference took place in Copenhagen, to which one young man and one young woman from each European country was invited. At this conference, the Plan of Action was refined, adopted and signed. It was then handed over to the Committee of Ministers of the Council of Europe and the EU Presidency as a concrete contribution from European youth to the EU Charter on Fundamental Rights. On a predetermined date, the country representatives will also hand over the plan to their respective parliaments.

Response to international initiatives

International initiatives are supported in a variety of ways and four examples of Government supported projects were found. The first two are examples of Denmark's involvement in European-wide initiatives while the latter two are examples of national initiatives with an international focus.

Associated Schools Project

Denmark joined the UNESCO Associated Schools Project (ASPnet) in 2000. Assisting collaborative work between participating schools in different countries and facilitating the exchange of information, resources, teachers and students is one of the main aims of this network. As part of their involvement in ASPnet, sixteen schools in Denmark, ranging from primary classes in the *folkeskole* to upper secondary schools, participate in the Transatlantic Slave Trade (TST) project and can exchange ideas, methods and staff with ASPnet schools in the other 156 countries participating in the network. This project aims to break the silence surrounding the Transatlantic Slave Trade and to improve the teaching of history by assisting a more comprehensive analysis of these events. This project is just one of about twelve flagship projects that include schools from different countries and that focus on specific educational topics, usually with an environmental or intercultural understanding focus. As Denmark only joined ASPnet in 2000 it has not yet had a wide impact in Danish schools.

European Schoolnet

European Schoolnet is a partnership of more than 20 European Ministries of Education where the internet is used to promote learning for teachers and students in schools across Europe. The website (www.eun.org) allows teachers and students to access information on international projects and also to become involved in web-based projects. Charting Coastal Pollution (The Copal Project) is one project that Danish students participate in along with students from France, Ireland, Norway and Scotland. Using scientifically recognised methods, students monitor and record the pollution in a stream, lake or stretch of beach, learn about the plant and animal life in these areas and exchange their findings with the other participant countries. In this way, students learn about the impact of human activities on the environment and are encouraged to reflect on how these might be reduced.

The Christmas Calendar
Each year NGOs are invited to nominate a project in a developing country as the focus for the Christmas Calendar. In the year 2000 the focus was on Mozambique and the project was the creation of local radio stations in the countryside. Films are made about the country and the project is broadcast on Danish television. Teaching materials are also developed. The money earned by selling the calendar is spent on the project. Close to €700,000 is raised each year.

Operation Daywork
Each year upper secondary students (aged 16–19) have a day off from their studies to do voluntary work for Operation Daywork. The money earned by the work is spent on a specific project in a developing country. A film and materials are made to inform the public about the project and the situation in that country. On average 50 per cent of students participate and they raise about €700,000.

Local authority support
The information we received about the extent of local authority support for global education initiatives was limited. Although no data were collected on specific initiatives supported at local authority level, it would appear that municipalities and individual schools are able to set specific objectives relating to global education. Although local authorities may promote global education in this way they do not generally appear to take a leading role. However, in each county there is an education resource centre and each centre has been asked to appoint an international consultant.

Global education in the school curriculum
While the Government determines the overall aims of education and the Minister of Education sets the targets for each subject, each local authority and school decides how those targets are to be attained. Curriculum guidelines are published for the individual subject areas

but these are seen purely as recommendations so are not mandatory for local school administrators. Schools are able to draw up their own curricula as long as they are in accordance with the aims and proficiency areas laid down by the Minister of Education.

The international dimension is a cross-curricular theme that is covered in most subject areas. The booklet *The International Dimension in the Subjects and Themes of the Folkeskole* (1998) summarises where in the curriculum references to the international dimension can be found. One respondent suggested that the lack of a clear context and definition for the international elements make systematic coverage difficult. Muller and Timm (2001) point out that the global dimension is not included as a cross-curricular theme in the *Folkeskole* Act 1994 in the same way as the three other dimensions (environment, creativity and information technology) are, nor is it highlighted in specific subject areas as being of particular importance.

Examples of good practice

Respondents indicated that there are many classroom materials on specific global education topics and that global education is also integrated into other themes and subjects. There are various organisations and institutions that offer support, advice and resources, including interactive websites. For example, the Danish Association for International Co-operation (MS) produces a quarterly newsletter on global education, a guest teacher database, library, consultants, teacher training courses, visits and pilot projects all aimed at enhancing global education (www.ms.dk).

The National Innovative Centre of General Education (SPF)

SPF consists of a school and a Youth Town. The school is a *folkeskole* given the task of developing innovative educational ideas including those relating to internationalisation and intercultural competence and caters for around 140 lower secondary pupils. The 20 or so staff members are mostly seconded from various municipalities and work in both the school and the Youth Town. The Youth Town is a training centre run jointly by business, NGOs and the Ministry of Education. It consists of a number of 'houses' within which various courses take place. These courses are usually one day long and the choice of courses available changes from year to year. Many of the courses have global education elements and include courses and materials about human rights, children's rights, the environment, democracy, conflict resolution and intercultural competence. These courses are available to students and teachers across Copenhagen and are attended by around 25,000 students each year. Courses are also provided to school students outside of the centre and in this way are accessed by about 100,000 students each year. More recently, courses have also been offered to teacher trainees.

Course examples:

- *The UN and the international community* focuses on the peace-keeping role of the UN and Denmark's role in UN activities.

- *From North to South* focuses on democracy, culture, language and identity in developing countries and in Denmark.

- *Children's Rights* focuses on the rights and conditions of children in various countries and in Denmark.

- *Ache-Human Rights at Stake* illustrate living and working conditions and the human rights situations of young people living in a poor country in the world today.

- *The Conflict Game* deals with national and international security policy, crisis management and conflict resolution.

Initial teacher training

In Denmark, teacher education is four years in duration and the entry requirements are the same as those for university. The Teacher Training Act 1998 states that international themes must be part of education wherever possible. This means that within all subject areas, consideration must now be given to how the international dimension can be incorporated. It is anticipated that this will have a significant impact on new teachers' understanding of global perspectives, making global issues part of daily teaching.

Several teacher training colleges have courses and projects focusing specifically on the global dimension. For example Ibis (an NGO), The National Innovative Centre, five teacher-training colleges in Denmark and three colleges in Namibia, South Africa and Nicaragua have been working on a project called *Intercultural Competence in Teacher Training*. This project involves training, the development of materials and methods, student exchanges and work experience. This work has been co-financed by the European Union and has resulted in a theoretical and a practical reader *Global Dimensions* published by MS and Ibis (www.ibis.dk).

Global education and the continuing professional development of teachers

There is no mandatory requirement for professional development on the international dimension. Respondents indicated that training courses relevant to the international dimension are provided by the Danish Pedagogical University and by various NGOs and resource centres. The Danish Pedagogical University, for example, provides part time courses, conferences and school development programmes that include global dimensions. One respondent pointed out that recent surveys indicate that these opportunities are not widely taken up by teachers:

> A lot of new material concerning global issues are collecting dust in the libraries and many courses offered to teachers by the resource centres are cancelled because of lack of applications.

In April 2001 the Danish Pedagogical University hosted a conference entitled *Citizenship, Adult Education and Lifelong Learning* as part of an international research project on adult education and democracy in partnership with the Association for World Education, the University of Western Cape, Cape Town and the UNESCO Institute for Education, Hamburg. This conference was attended by teachers and teacher educators, many of then working in informal and adult settings, from a number of countries in Europe, Africa, Asia and North America (Korsgaard *et al.*, 2001). The Association for World Citizenship publishes a journal on various aspects of global education entitled the *Journal for World Education*.

NGO networks and activities

NGOs play an important role in Denmark's development assistance and are financed largely by government. They are represented on the Danida board and are also involved in policy formation. The national platform for NGOs involved in global education, *Faglig Forum*, acts as an umbrella organisation for NGOs engaged in development education (www.u-land.dk). It has almost 40 member organisations (for example ADRA Denmark, AFS Interculture, Amnesty International, the Children's Fund Denmark, Danish Centre for Culture and Development, Danish Refugee Council, Danish Youth Council, Danish Centre for Human Rights, Danish Association for International Co-operation, Red Cross Youth).

These NGOs support and promote the international dimension by lobbying the Ministry of Education, by producing and supplying materials and resource personnel and by supporting and co-ordinating various projects. One respondent noted that many of the Danish NGOs publish interesting and stimulating materials that can be used in cross-curricular activities and project work. Many Danish NGOs co-operated in publishing the book *Around the Globe in 45 minutes*, where most of the existing global education material can be found. This publication is also available on a website thus making it accessible to a wide audience.

Faglig Forum has expressed concern to the Minister of Education about the lack of global education in the *folkeskole* curriculum and has proposed five recommendations:

- global dimension should be a compulsory cross-curricular theme in education

- the appointment of advisors on the global dimension in the Ministry of Education

- the new Danish Centre for International Education Activities prioritise the global dimension

- teacher training should address the global dimension and intercultural competence

- the Ministry of Education and the Department of International Development Co-operation (within the Ministry of Foreign Affairs) co-ordinate their support for the global dimension at all educational levels (Muller and Timm, 2001).

Project example: Action 21

From January through to December 1998, 100 classes in Danish schools and 100 classes and clubs in Zimbabwe took part in Action 21 activities. The project aimed to promote environmental education with 14 to 17-year-olds through intercultural dialogue. Strengthening students' environmental consciousness and developing their action competence were important aspects of the programme. For teachers, the project involved the establishment of teacher networks, project related training and the development of new educational materials. Students became involved in club and class activities where they learned about environmental and development issues in both countries. They also took part in local community investigations and exchanged information and ideas about how a sustainable environment can be created. There were also visits from Zimbabwean teachers. The project was supported by a number of NGOs (Danish Association for International Co-operation; Geographers' Union, Danish UN Association; AFS Interculture; Danish Open Air Council). The formal evaluation of the project indicated that both teachers and pupils perceived the programme to be more a cultural than an environmental programme. Pupils, for example, reported finding the correspondence with partners in Zimbabwe and getting to know more about the youth of Zimbabwe as the most exciting part of Action 21.

Research and publications

The Danish Pedagogical University was reported to carry out some research in global education both at national and regional levels. Denmark's Pedagogical Institute (DPU) was also cited as researching in this area. The Danish United Nations Association and Education (*FN-forbundet og undervismingen*) (Buttenschon, 1998) is a research project focusing on the current status and application of global education in primary and secondary schools in Denmark and

includes an analysis of institutional support at various levels including initial teacher training.

Action 21: An Evaluation (Larsen *et al.*, 1999) reports on the formal
evaluation of the Action 21 project and is based on both qualitative
and quantitative data. It describes and analyses the prerequisites and
possibilities for developing action competence. The author suggests
that both teacher readiness and the school's organisational culture
can present hurdles to the development of global competence but
that pupils generally have the desire and inclination to work with
global subjects and partners. He argues that the development of
greater global action competence among teachers will require
further input in both pre-service and in-service settings.

Action Competence between Individualisation and Globalisation
(Larsen, 2000) develops the theme of action competence, exploring
the relationship between individual action and globalisation processes, using the Action 21 project to illustrate some of its points. It
explores ways in which the teaching of global dimensions in schools
has changed in both content and process since the 1960s. Specifically, it discusses the move from an ethnocentric, didactic approach to one that is much more culturally divergent and reliant on
multiple approaches to teaching and learning.

Figure 3.1 highlights some key strengths, weaknesses, and opportunities, as well as some potential threats for global education within
the Danish system, as identified by our Danish respondents. A comparative analysis of the four country case studies is developed in
chapter seven.

Figure 3.1: Strengths, weaknesses, opportunities, threats (SWOT) to GE in Denmark

Strengths	Weakness
Formal recognition of the importance of the international dimension in the *Folkeskole* Act which lays the foundation for greater possibilities in relation to global education than in the past.	Lack of direct and explicit guidelines about how various elements of the international dimension might be incorporated into day-to-day teaching.
Availability of a diverse range of global education related materials.	Policy on its own does not change practice. It will take time for the spirit of the *Folkeskole* Act to be fully put into practice.
Partnerships and co-operation between various organisations in promoting global education.	Heavy dependence by NGOs on government funding.
Tradition of democracy in education.	
Opportunities	**Threats**
The creation of a network consisting of five NGOs, SPF, five teacher training colleges, five resource centres and ten schools and an attached researcher.	The international dimension is just one of a number of areas that teachers are expected to include in their teaching (i.e. alongside the green dimension, the creative dimension and the information technology dimension).
Some of the objectives of this network are:	
• Increase teachers' awareness of the world of possibilities offered by global issues and the organizations' wide range of materials and projects	
• Find out what it takes to ensure that GE is implemented in schools	
• Uncover the needs of the teachers and students concerning GE	
• Find out where and when global teaching really makes a difference.	

4
England

England, the largest of our case study countries, has a population of 49 million, constituting more than four fifths of the total population of the UK. One of the peculiar features of the UK is the absence of a written constitution. There has, however, been significant constitutional reform at the turn of the century, with devolution of government in Scotland and Wales and the introduction of the Human Rights Act 1998, which incorporates the European Convention on Human Rights into UK law. The establishment of a Scottish Parliament and Welsh Assembly and the development of a new political settlement in Northern Ireland have led to increased interest and debate on what it means to be British. The introduction of a directly elected mayor for London marks a step towards the setting up of English regional authorities. These developments have caused individuals and groups to consider how citizenship is related to national and regional identities. So, for example, what does it mean to be British and Scottish or to be British and English? Meanings of nationality and national identity are being re-examined and re-defined.

Just 3.8 per cent of the population of the UK is classified as foreign or foreign born, according to OECD statistics. As in the Netherlands, these figures do not reveal the extent of cultural diversity within the country. Questions on ethnicity are asked in the UK census, allowing us to make estimates concerning the ethnic make-up of the population. We therefore have data indicating the extent of cultural diversity, which would not be revealed by country of birth, since Britain experienced significant immigration from former colonies, notably from the Caribbean and the Indian subcontinent, in the two decades after the Second World War. Most of these former migrants and their families have British citizenship. Minorities constitute around 11 per cent of the population in England. Estimates for 1998 suggest that the largest minority group is Irish (4 per cent), followed by those classifying themselves as Indian, Pakistani and Bangladeshi (totalling 3.4 per cent), African-Caribbean (1.6 per cent), African (0.7 per cent) and Chinese (0.3 per cent) (Parekh, 2000a).

In the year 2000, 125,000 people were accepted for settlement in the UK. The largest proportion were from Asia (38 per cent), with migrants from the Indian sub-continent constituting nearly half of this group, followed by Africa (36 per cent), European countries which are not EU members states (12 per cent), and the Americas (9 per cent). Of these, 24,800 were those granted refugee status. This represents an increase of 18,200 from 1998, which the Government explains largely in terms of the processing of a backlog of applications from previous years (Dudley and Harvey, 2001).

A Government White Paper on nationality, immigration and asylum, published in February 2002, proposes that those seeking British citizenship should be able to demonstrate competence in English. It also proposes there be a citizenship ceremony, at which new citizens be required to swear an oath of allegiance (Home Office, 2002). Similar ceremonies exist in other EU states, such as France and Austria, although attendance is not compulsory. Public and media debates about refugees and asylum seekers, and the processes through which new citizens pass, influence the wider debates about identity and citizenship.

In 1999 the UK spent 0.24 per cent of GDP on Overseas Development Aid, which is the lowest of the case study countries. It aims to increase this percentage to 0.33 by 2003/4. Since 1997 the Government has funded a public awareness campaign to increase understanding of international development issues in an effort to raise the level of charitable donations and tackle poverty.

A survey of the attitudes of the citizens of the European Union towards minority groups suggests that in the UK support for policies aimed at improving social coexistence between members of minority groups is similar to the EU average. 22 per cent of British people are classified as actively tolerant and supportive of antiracist policies and a further 36 per cent are classified as passively tolerant. 15 per cent are classified as intolerant, displaying strong negative attitudes towards minorities, and the rest (27 per cent) are ambivalent. There is, however, a lower level of acceptance where refugees and asylum seekers are concerned. According to the survey, multicultural optimism is decreasing in the UK. In 2000, there is less agreement than there was in 1997 with the statement that it is a good thing for any society to be made up of people of different races, religions and cultures. Furthermore, fewer people concur with the statement that a country's diversity in terms of race, religion and culture adds to its strength. At the same time, the demand for the 'repatriation' of migrants is increasing. As in Ireland, the picture may be distorted by the fact that a high number of people were not willing to respond to certain questions, leading the researchers to conclude that the picture painted by the survey may be more optimistic than the reality (Thalhammer *et al.*, 2001).

In 1999 the report of the Stephen Lawrence Inquiry identified institutional racism as a feature of British public life. The report of the inquiry made 70 recommendations, of which three addressed education, which were broadly accepted by the Government. The report of the Stephen Lawrence inquiry defined institutional racism as:

> The collective failure of an organisation to provide an appropriate and professional service to people because of their colour, culture, or ethnic origin. It can be seen or detected in processes, attitudes and behaviour which amount to discrimination through unwitting prejudice, ignorance, thoughtlessness and racist stereotyping which disadvantage minority ethnic people (Macpherson *et al.*, 1999).

Education policy: an overview

In England, education is compulsory between the ages of 5 and 16. The organisation of schooling varies between local education authorities but in general primary schools provide education through to Year 6 and secondary schools from Years 7 to 11. Increasing numbers of children are provided with a nursery school place from the age of three or four. At 16 plus, most students continue with some form of education or training, following two or three year courses either in a college or at school. The Government has set a target to expand university education, aiming to provide places for 50 per cent of young people by 2010.

Until the 1990s, schools had considerable freedom to develop their own curricula, the only constraints being preparation for public examinations at 16 plus, and the statutory requirement to teach religious education. The Education Reform Act 1988 marked a significant change in the control of schools, although earlier Education Acts during the 1980s had already indicated a change in policy direction. Throughout the 1990s there have been a series of Education Acts which have transformed the context in which schools work. Schools have been given increasing control over their own budgets and local education authorities (LEAs) have seen many of their former responsibilities disappear. School governing bodies now have significant decision-making powers. At the same time, the curriculum has come under tighter central government control. A national curriculum for England was introduced in the 1990s and has also been subject to various revisions and reforms. The most recent of these took place in the year 2000, following the election of a Labour government in 1997. In comparison with Denmark and the Netherlands, England has a tightly prescribed National Curriculum, although the most recent reforms allow for more flexibility and teacher control than existed in the early 1990s. The most significant new development has been the introduction of Citizenship as a statutory subject for secondary schools from 2002. Education provision at both school and local authority levels is monitored by the national school inspection agency, OFSTED.

The Government acknowledges that there remain wide variations in both educational provision and outcomes between schools and between different regions. For example, the 2001 Education White Paper argues that:

> there is still more to do to tackle problems at the minority of schools – and education authorities – that are still failing pupils and parents.

We must also drive up standards at those schools which, while not failing, perform well below the national average.

... almost one in four secondary schools still lacks the physical capacity to teach the basics effectively. Similarly, Information and Communications Technology (ICT) in schools has been very significantly improved, but we are yet to take full advantage of the potential of new technology (DfES, 2001: 8 and 9: 2.4 and 2.7).

One of the particular challenges is to address the problems which are causing young people from particular ethnic groups to perform, on average, below the standards of their peers. Examples of the effects of institutional racism within the education system have been well documented. They include the over-representation of black and other minority students among those excluded from school (Osler, 1997b; DfEE, 1999); differentials in educational outcomes between ethnic groups in many schools and local education authorities (Gillborn and Gipps, 1996; Richardson and Wood, 1999); and the barriers to promotion and career progression which black and minority teachers may experience at each stage in their careers, whether they are in training, newly qualified, or holding headships or other senior positions (Osler, 1997a). Although schools are clearly implicated in institutional racism they are also seen, in the Stephen Lawrence Inquiry report, as part of the solution and are required to address and prevent racism.

Ministry of Education initiatives

The government department responsible for education in England is the Department for Education and Skills (DfES). Other key agencies are the Qualifications and Curriculum Authority (QCA) which provides curriculum guidance to schools, the Teacher Training Agency (TTA) which sets out the basic teacher training curriculum, and OFSTED, the school inspection agency.

In England the National Curriculum underwent considerable revision in 2000. The most significant new development of Curriculum 2000 is the introduction of citizenship education as an additional curriculum subject. Citizenship is a statutory subject in secondary schools (Years 7-11: ages 11-16) from 2002 and is also to be taught in primary schools, together with Personal, Social and Health Education (PSHE). The DfES also set up a working group on Citizenship 16-19 and programmes of citizenship education for those aged 16-19 have been developed.

The Learning and Skills Council (LSC) for post-16 sixteen education and training includes Education for Sustainable Development (ESD) in its remit. At both primary and secondary levels provision of citizenship education will be monitored through the school inspection system. Although the QCA has published guidance for schools on citizenship, it is probably fair to say that global citizenship is not yet widely recognised as a central feature of this new curriculum subject. The DfES has, however, endorsed (and part funded) an NGO publication entitled *Citizenship Education: the global dimension* (DEA, 2001). This guidance booklet for teachers looks at how the global dimension is part of all aspects of citizenship. Although it was not distributed to all schools there is a considerable demand for this publication. The DfES does not provide schools with detailed guidance on anti-racism, although there has been, since 2000, an explicit values statement for the National Curriculum which is compatible with the aims of global education:

> Equality of opportunity is one of the broad set of common values which underpin the school curriculum and the work of schools. These include a commitment to valuing ourselves, other families and other relationships, the wider groups to which we belong, the diversity of our society and the environment in which we live (DfEE, 1999: 4).

In spring 2002 the QCA launched guidelines and an interactive website for teachers to demonstrate how schools might value diversity and challenge racism within the framework of the national curriculum. www.qca.org.uk.

Curriculum 2000 makes explicit reference to global society and sustainable development in its aims and purposes and also in relation to specific subject areas. Most significantly, the ministry published guidance to schools on *Developing a Global Dimension in the School Curriculum* (DfEE, 2000). This was produced in co-operation with the Department for International Development and the NGO sector. It is aimed at both primary and secondary schools and sets out to illustrate how a global dimension can be incorporated into the formal school curriculum and 'into the wider life of the school' through what is referred to as the informal curriculum or school ethos. It highlights eight key concepts which it identifies as central to learning about global issues:

- Citizenship
- Sustainable development
- Social justice
- Values and perceptions
- Diversity
- Interdependence
- Conflict resolution
- Human rights.

Commenting upon the guidelines, the director of the Development Education Centre, Birmingham, links global understanding to citizens' responsibilities in their own locality and stresses the interconnectedness of local national and global issues:

> Development education is important to our own citizenship, and to our local governance. It is about working towards the understanding that local and national governments take account of their global responsibilities, and recognising not only that everything we do impacts on others, but equally, that everything that goes on in the world affects us. ... People increasingly understand that development awareness is an essential part of the dynamic of change rather than an optional extra (Sinclair, 2000).

The Government has highlighted citizenship education as a key means by which education for racial equality can be achieved (Home Office, 1999). Racism has been identified as serving to undermine democracy in Europe and needs to be addressed through programmes in schools and in teacher education (Council of Europe, 1985). Citizenship education in England is seen, as it is across Europe, as a means of strengthening democracy and therefore of challenging racism as an anti-democratic force (see for example, Osler, Rathenow and Starkey 1996; Holden and Clough, 1998). The Government sees citizenship education as a key means by which race equality initiatives will be developed in the curriculum.

The school inspection agency, OFSTED, came under sharp criticism from the Commission for Racial Equality for its failure to monitor how schools are addressing and preventing racism (Osler and Morrison, 2000), something which it was charged to do by Government (Home Office, 1999), following the publication of the report of the Stephen Lawrence Inquiry. It has since published guidance on 'educational inclusion' which includes a number of equal opportunities issues, including those of gender and race, and required that all inspectors contracted to OFSTED undergo mandatory training on educational inclusion by September 2001. From 2002 OFSTED has a legal obligation to monitor how schools are fulfilling their duty to promote race equality under the Race Relations (Amendment) Act 2000.

Other Ministry initiatives

Two other Government departments play a key role in aspects of global education. The Department for International Development (DFID) promotes development education and awareness. Its development awareness budget for 2001 is £6.5 million, which has risen from just under £0.75 million in 1997. Organisations wishing to access this budget are required to submit proposals against explicit criteria which address the Government's international development targets, which were set out in the 1997 White Paper *Eliminating World Poverty: a challenge for the 21st century* and confirmed in the 2000 White Paper *Eliminating World Poverty: making globalisation work for the poor*. The targets, which focus on poverty reduction, are:

- A reduction by one half of people living in extreme poverty by 2015

- Universal primary education in all countries by 2015

- Demonstrated progress towards gender equality and the empowerment of women by eliminating gender disparity in primary and secondary education by 2005

- Access to reproductive health services for all individuals of appropriate ages as soon as possible and not later than 2015

• The implementation of national strategies for sustainable development in all countries by 2005, to ensure that the loss of environmental resources is effectively reversed at global and national levels by 2015.

One of the key contributions of DFID is to provide a UK database of resources and sources of support for schools wishing to develop a global dimension to their curriculum. The database, which can be found at www.globaldimension.org.uk , has been prepared by a team at the Centre for Citizenship Studies in Education (CCSE) and includes over 500 entries. It enables teachers to locate resources by curriculum area, topic or issue, subject, geographical region and age group. The database is linked to the National Grid for Learning (NGFL). DFID has published a strategy document *Building Support for Development* (DFID, 1999) which builds upon the 1997 White Paper and identifies the following priority areas in which development awareness might be addressed: formal education, the media, business and trade unions, churches and other faith groups. This document forms the base line against which proposals for development awareness funding across the UK are judged by DFID. The department has also published a consultation paper *Enabling Effective Support* which 'recognises that young people should have an entitlement to development education and reflects the priority DFID has given to development education work in schools' (DFID, 2000).

DFID is also working closely with colleagues in UK University Departments of Education to ensure that the global dimension of education is adequately covered in the new citizenship curricula. A publication, produced jointly by DfES, DFID, and a consortium of NGOs addresses global perspectives in initial teacher education (DEA, 2002 forthcoming). DFID is a member of a consortium which will ensure that resources and support are available to help teachers teach the Citizenship curriculum from a global perspective. The department has also co-operated with the DfES, the ministries of education in the other constituent parts of the UK, and leading development education bodies to publish guidance documents on how the global dimension can be incorporated into the curriculum and the wider life of schools (see section on Ministry of Education initiatives above). These documents have been distributed to every local education authority in England. DFID also places considerable emphasis on school linking.

The Department of the Environment, Food and Rural Affairs (DEFRA), together with DfES, has set up a panel which makes recommendations to government on all aspects of education and awareness of sustainable development. The panel's report *Education for Sustainable Development: more relevant than ever* (DETR, 2001) makes recommendations to central, regional and local government, analysing needs in schools, further and higher education, workplaces and the professions, the youth service and general public. It argues that:

- all schools should have local authority support to provide Education for Sustainable Development (ESD) and have a policy on becoming a sustainable institution

- all pupils should acquire knowledge to enable them to participate in the achievement of sustainable development

- all initial and continuing training for teachers, governors, nursery staff and childminders should have ESD integrated throughout.

It recommends that the Government:

- creates more support and guidance for ESD in the DfEE (now DfES) and DETR (now DEFRA)

- considers how the professional needs of teachers be met in this area

- requires all schools to have a policy on sustainable development

- produces a circular on schools as sustainable institutions.

The report goes on to make specific recommendations to QCA, OFSTED, the TTA and the General Teaching Council to support these goals.

Interestingly, legislation introduced by the Home Office is likely to have a key impact on schools, requiring them, in effect, to develop antiracist curricula. The Race Relations (Amendment) Act 2000, which places a duty on all public bodies, including schools, to promote race equality, will require schools to review their curricula to ensure it is in keeping with this objective (Osler, 2002).

Response to international initiatives

When the UK re-joined UNESCO in 1987 it did not renew its membership of the UNESCO Associated Schools project (ASPnet). In 2000 DFID reviewed the position. Its report concluded that only a few schools had benefited from the project in the past. Those countries which have most successfully developed projects within ASPnet have invested resources in a national co-ordinator and support structures. In the UK, government-funded organisations such as the Central Bureau for International Education and Training are enabling and supporting schools to develop international links and in other global education initiatives. There are therefore no plans to rejoin the ASPnet project in the immediate future.

At the Council of Europe Vienna Summit held in 1993, Heads of State and Government, persuaded that 'manifestations of intolerance threaten democratic societies and their basic values' called for a

> ... broad European Youth Campaign to mobilise the public in favour of a tolerant society based on the equal dignity of all its members and against manifestations of racism, xenophobia, antisemitism and intolerance (Council of Europe, Vienna Declaration, 1993).

Although initiatives in response to such campaigns are undertaken by some schools and local authorities, our respondents were not clear that there exist clear mechanisms for communicating international initiatives, such as those of the Council of Europe and other bodies, to schools and local authorities. The British Council has a growing role, for example, through its global citizenship team and co-ordination of the *On the Line* millennium project.

Local authority support

It appears that local authorities are generally supportive of global education, although such general support may not necessarily be translated into concrete practices. Some aspects of global education undertaken in LEAs, notably multicultural and antiracist work, are externally inspected and monitored by OFSTED and LEA performance is reported upon.

Many local authorities have carried out important work related to Agenda 21 and sustainable development. For example, in Birmingham activities have been carried out with local schools in the *Learning Today with Tomorrow in Mind* project (DEC, 2000b). Three of the organisations which worked with the local authority and with local schools were an environmental education centre in the inner city, the Black Environmental Network, and the local botanical gardens. Projects focused on recycling, plants, and how schools might become sustainable communities.

Another example of a joint local authority and non-governmental global education project is the Forward Thinking initiative between Birmingham LEA and Birmingham Development Education Centre. However, an evaluation of this work suggests that it is the NGO which is the partner most engaged in this initiative (DEC, 1998, 1999 and 2000a). Some local authorities (for example Somerset, Croydon) have received funding from DFID to work with NGOs to promote global dimensions in education while others work within their Education Departments. (For example Tower Hamlets works with the local Humanities Education Centre on a project on *Global Footprints*.)

Global education in the school curriculum

Traditionally, multicultural education in England has focused on the cultural and on issues of identity. In practice, many schools have avoided political and structural questions when dealing with the here and now. Such issues have often been reserved for history and geography lessons. Students' cultural development has therefore often taken place in a political vacuum. The new Citizenship curriculum places considerable emphasis on 'political literacy'. Political literacy is defined as 'pupils learning about and how to make themselves effective in public life through knowledge, skills and values' (QCA, 1998: 41). The emphasis on political literacy within the Crick Report opens up a new opportunity to develop a more rounded curriculum, where questions of identity and cultural development are balanced with a knowledge and understanding of human rights and democratic practice (Osler and Starkey, 1996 and 2000).

The Crick Report suggests that at the end of primary school (year 6, age 11), and in the context of understanding the world as a global community, pupils are expected to know the meaning of:

poverty
famine
disease
charity
aid
human rights.

By the end of Year 9 (age 14) students are expected, in the context of human rights, to know the meaning of:

prejudice
xenophobia
discrimination
pluralism
and, at the end of Year 11 (age 16), civil rights.

Examples of good practice

The United Nations Association (UK) has produced a pack *Citizenship, Participation and Action: the United Nations* to support the Citizenship curriculum and enable groups of schools to work together to run a day-long simulation: the Model United Nations General Assembly (MUNGA).

This pack provides schools with a pack with everything they might need to organise a model United Nations General Assembly, for groups of up to 100 secondary school students. A UN meeting can be modelled within one class, a year group or with other schools. Small groups of participants (usually three) are assigned a Member State of the UN. They assume the role of that country's diplomats or delegates at whichever UN body is being enacted. Before the event the delegates research their country's position on the selected topics. The topics can be selected to explore any global challenge, such as HIV/AIDs, third world debt, poverty in cities. The delegations come together and enact the UN meeting. The pack provides guidance for organisers, reference materials for teachers and students, briefings for delegates and specific country briefings, from a wide range of countries (www.una-uk.org). The simulations permit participants to gain an understanding of the UN and its processes and the influence of individual nations within the UN framework (Tennant, 2001).

A number of innovative projects have been undertaken by the Centre for Global and Development Education (GLADE) in Somerset. GLADE:

- maintains a development education, multicultural and anti-racist resource centre

- provides support for teachers and students on a wide range of global and development issues (classroom support, in-service training, advice, exhibitions, initiating and undertaking action projects)

- produces a range of resources for classroom use and several guides for in-service training.

Examples of GLADE projects include:

Common Threads On the Line

The UNESCO *On the Line* project focused on global citizenship and sustainable development by looking at life in the countries of Europe and West Africa that lie on the Meridian line. In Somerset, 40 schools participated by exploring the common threads of people living on the line and then producing a lengthy tapestry depicting aspects of life in the eight countries along the Meridian line. The tapestry then provided the focus for a *Common Threads On the Line* celebration day where schools and other visitors enjoyed the artwork.

Children's Rights Calendar

During the autumn of 2000, twelve different youth organisations participated in children's rights sessions run by a GLADE staff member. Guided by a local artist, each group then produced artwork around the theme 'Children's Rights' which were subsequently photographed and combined to produce the Children's Rights Calendar.

The Global Citizen

This is an activity-based quarterly publication produced by GLADE to support the Citizenship curriculum in secondary schools and was developed in response to requests from local teachers. Each issue focuses on a single global development topic and contains student activities and information that relates that topic to the everyday lives of students. Topics covered have included the World Trade Organisation, Aid, fair trade and tourism. GLADE aims to distribute this magazine to all secondary schools in Somerset.

Initial teacher training

From September 2001, four universities are providing initial teacher training for students wishing to specialise in becoming teachers of Citizenship in secondary schools. A number of others are introducing citizenship as a second subject for trainees. It is not yet clear to what extent global education is a feature of this training. The TTA has published guidelines on the achievement of ethnic minority pupils which addresses aspects of anti-racist and multicultural training (TTA, 2000). The Development Education Association has published two documents *A Framework for the International Dimension for Schools in England* (1999) and *Training Teachers for Tomorrow* (1998). The first provides guidance to schools and the second offers practical suggestions on how a global dimension might be incorporated into the initial teacher training curriculum. It addresses the notion of the active global citizen who is willing to participate in public life, and who is open to others' cultures and ideas, is committed to gender and racial equality and to maintaining and enhancing the integrity and biodiversity of the natural environment. The DEA introduced a major programme of in-service training for development education practitioners in 2002. Some NGOs run sessions at local universities for trainee teachers. One example is the work undertaken by MUNDI in Nottingham. Another example of NGO partnership in initial teacher training is the Global Education Project run by the World Studies Trust which is working with eight universities to provide training in global education.

Continuing professional development of teachers

Teachers in England have no formal entitlement to continuing professional development, though a number of opportunities are available. Thus it is a question of individuals or schools prioritising global education in their personal or institutional development plans. A number of university departments of education offer short training courses, often leading to some form of accreditation in particular aspects of global education. For example, a number are providing courses in citizenship education for teachers in their locality and from 2000 the Centre for Citizenship Studies in Education (CCSE) has offered a distance course *Learning for Citizenship*. It deals with some but not all aspects of global education, with a strong emphasis on cultural diversity and racial justice. CCSE also runs a programme of training for teachers wishing to introduce a global dimension into their work and has a resource centre for teachers of global education materials. The University of Hertfordshire, South Bank University and the Institute of Education at the University of London also run modules and courses that promote global dimensions.

NGO networks and activities

The Development Education Association is an umbrella body for around 250 NGOs and other organisations engaged in promoting education on public understanding of global and development issues. It sees the development agenda as being at the heart of the global dimension and has produced a *Principles and Practice* document (2000) for those engaged in development education with schools. The aim is to bring global perspectives into the mainstream. Although there is an emphasis on environmental education and education for sustainable development, the links with multicultural education and anti-racist education organisations and networks are not as strong. The DEA is however working with a range of black community organisations looking at black perspectives in development education following Ohri's (1997) report.

The Education in Human Rights Network was founded in 1988 to bring together NGOs and academics to promote the human rights education agenda of the Council of Europe. It publishes a regular newsletter. The Council for Environmental Education is an umbrella body for organisations working in environment education. NGO publications that support global education include a briefing paper on religious education and citizenship produced by Christian Aid and a guidance booklet on human rights produced by the DEA and the Education in Human Rights Network.

Academic research and publications

The various elements that contribute to global education have received varying degrees of attention from researchers. From 1998 to 2000 the Economic and Social Research Council (ESRC) sponsored a research seminar series addressing *Human Rights and Democracy in Schools*. (For further information visit the Centre for Citizenship Studies in Education website: www.le.ac.uk/education/centres/citizenship.) The seminar series enjoyed the technical support of the Council of Europe and, although it focused on developments in the UK, including the impact of the Human Rights Act 1998 on human rights education, it also reflected a number of international perspectives. One key outcome was the publication of a collection of papers *Citizenship and Democracy in Schools* (Osler, 2000), which addresses questions of citizenship in the context of cultural diversity and race equality.

We argue that in its representation of minorities, and in its discussion of identity and diversity, the new Citizenship curriculum is, in many ways, inadequate. Nevertheless, the introduction of a new citizenship curriculum provides us with a unique opportunity to promote education for racial equality. We argue that we need to build upon the concept of a political literacy as it is presented in the Crick Report and demonstrate how a commitment to human rights principles and skills for challenging racism are essential features of a politically literate citizen within a democratic society (Osler, 1999, Osler 2000c, Osler and Starkey, 2000).

Research into citizenship education has also been a key focus of the National Foundation for Educational Research (NFER), which is a government-funded institution. The West Midlands Global Citizenship Commission is working with the University of Birmingham to develop research and publications in this field (see, for example, Carter, Harber and Serf, 2002). Other research is reported in the

Development Education Journal. Calvert (2001) presents the Government's perspective on key challenges in this area for the next five years while a recent DEA (undated) document reflects on current development education trends in England. The DEA is focusing on evaluation in an attempt to assess the effectiveness of global and development education initiatives.

Figure 4.1 highlights strengths, weaknesses and opportunities as well as threats to global education in England.

Figure 4.1: Strengths, weaknesses, opportunities, threats (SWOT) to GE in England

Strengths	Weaknesses
Formal recognition at central government level of the importance of GE and good support from government via DFID.	Global citizenship still not widely recognised as a central feature of the new citizenship curriculum.
The existence of the DEA and a well-established network of NGOs that support and promote certain aspects of GE – as with the network of DECs.	Limited government guidance to schools on anti-racism. Little emphasis on GE within teacher training.
Introduction of citizenship education as an additional mandatory subject from 2002.	Insufficient support for GE within the DfES.
Availability of a good range of resources that promote aspects of GE.	
Opportunities	**Threats**
Increasing use of ICT (e.g. GE related websites including databases).	Marginalisation – GE still not part of 'essential learning' for all students –
New developments in initial teacher training and continuing professional development of teachers.	DE, ESD, GE – still not widely used terms within the education mainstream.
Race Relations (Amendment) Act 2000 requiring schools to promote race equality.	

5

Republic of Ireland

Ireland has traditionally been a relatively homogenous society, with a strong tradition of solidarity with the developing world and concern for global issues. The country has gone through a period of rapid economic and demographic change in recent years, experiencing a period of boom and a considerable growth in the number of immigrants, including refugees and asylum seekers. The population is now more than 3.7 million, the highest on record since 1881. Ireland also has a relatively young population, in relation to previous decades and to other European countries; 41 per cent is under the age of 25.

The 1990s saw the emergence of the 'Celtic Tiger' economy – one of the fastest growing in the world and one which produced a dramatic growth in GDP: the average annual growth rate between 1996 and 2000 was 9.24 per cent (Department of Foreign Affairs, undated). The decade saw a fall in unemployment from 15.2 per cent in 1989 to 5.8 per cent in 1999 and a move away from an agriculturally based economy to one that is dominated by information and communications technology. These changes are reflected in the move from a rurally based population to a more urbanised one and in an increase in the numbers of European Union (EU) and other migrants to Ireland.

These changes, together with important political developments arising from the Good Friday Agreement, designed to achieve a new settlement between the Republic of Ireland, Great Britain and Northern Ireland, have promoted debate and reflection about Irish national identity:

> The economic boom, while bringing many welcome features, has pre-
> sented serious challenges for a people who previously created a
> national identity out of being Catholic, impoverished, agrarian, and
> primed for emigration (Hammond et al., 2001: 3).

A once relatively homogeneous society is now a multicultural society. While close to half of Ireland's immigrants during the 1990s were Irish nationals returning home, the rest are drawn from very diverse groups, representing over 160 different nationalities. In 1999, 3.1 per cent of the population were classed as foreign or foreign born. EU citizens formed 62 per cent of immigrants in 2000 with British nationals making up nearly two thirds of this number. Beyond the EU, the highest number of immigrants were first from China and then the United States. In the same year more than 18,000 work permits were issued, which represented a 300 per cent increase on the previous year. Nearly 11,000 people from 98 different countries applied for refugee status. Most asylum applications came from people originating in Nigeria, Romania, the Czech Republic, Moldova and the Congo. Travellers, with an estimated population of 22,000, are still the largest minority group in Ireland but the gap is narrowing. There is a long established Jewish community and grow-ing Muslim and Chinese communities (Department of the Taoiseach, 2001; National Anti-Racism Awareness Programme, 2001).

A Europe-wide survey confirms that Irish attitudes towards minorities are broadly similar to the attitudes of other Europeans. Irish respondents were more likely than others to agree that minority groups should be given preferential treatment. There is, however, some cause for concern. Racial tensions have increased as demo-graphic changes have taken place. In 1997, 16 per cent of those questioned tended to agree that the presence of people from minority groups offered grounds for insecurity. Three years later, the per-centage of those who agreed with this view had increased to 42 per cent. A significant number of Irish respondents were unwilling to give their views on particular questions, which leads researchers to conclude that the findings may present an overly optimistic view of attitudes to minorities in Ireland (Thalhammer et al., 2001). Studies show that hostility to Travellers remains deeply entrenched and

- The Human Rights Commission

- The Equality Authority (EA)

- The National Consultative Committee on Racism and Interculturalism (NCCRI)

The Human Rights Commission was formally established in July 2001. It is an independent body that aims to promote, protect and develop human rights in the Republic and (jointly with the Northern Ireland Human Rights Commission) across the whole of Ireland. It also has an international role through its participation in European and international human rights events. In partial fulfilment of this responsibility it will undertake or sponsor research and educational activities in the field (Department of Justice, Equality and Law Reform, 2001).

The Equality Authority is a statutory body set up in 1998. It is responsible for a broad equality agenda and has the overall aim of working towards elimination of discrimination in employment and the promotion of equal opportunities. It has a board whose members are drawn from employer and employee organisations and from organisations with experience in equality issues.

The NCCRI is a specialised advisory body to the Department of Justice, set up in 1999. It brings together governmental and non-governmental organisations to address racism and promote a multi-cultural society. NCCRI works in partnership with some 20 organisations and it is networked with over 300 organisations engaged in challenging racism in Ireland.

In October 2001, the Irish government launched *National Anti-Racism Awareness*, an antiracist programme aimed at raising public awareness about racism and supporting the 'development of a multi-cultural society free of discrimination against minorities' (Depart-ment of the Taoiseach, 2001). This constitutes just one part of a more comprehensive programme aimed at promoting greater equality and inclusion in an increasingly multicultural Ireland.

Response to international initiatives

In contrast with one of the 1995 Education White Paper's stated aims, our respondents viewed Government support of international initiatives promoting global education as relatively weak. One suggested that it is difficult to assess how well informed schools are about international initiatives and thought that it is mainly through NGOs and trade union newsletters rather than Government that schools obtain information.

Nevertheless, several examples of international projects supported by Government were identified. These include:

- NSC World Aware Education Award (supported by NCDE)

- Council of Europe Education for Democratic Citizenship project

- UNESCO Associated Schools Project (ASPnet) (supported by DES)

- Europe at School Competition (supported by DES).

Government support for such initiatives was seen to be increasing and it was also noted that some European policy statements are disseminated through bodies, such as the NCCRI, on which the DES is represented.

Europe at School Competition

This secondary school art and essay competition is supported by the Council of Europe, the European Parliament, the European Commission and the European Cultural Foundation. Approximately 40 countries take part. The competition, which has a different theme each year, aims to promote European understanding among pupils and teachers. Ireland has been involved in the Europe at School Competition since 1968. The DES supports this initiative by ensuring that information inviting schools to take part are sent to every secondary school and by advertising the competition on the Departmental website.

Environmental Achievement Awards programme

Since 1998, many primary and secondary schools in Ireland have registered on the Environmental Achievement Awards Programme for Schools (formerly known as the Green Flag Programme for Schools). This is a Europe-wide project designed to encourage and acknowledge whole-school action for the environment. It is a flexible programme with different schools finding different ways of achieving Green School status. Examples of projects that have already been undertaken are provided in the guidance and include:

- A recycling sale of work and the production of an environmental play in order to purchase a paper shredder for the reuse of newspaper as animal bedding

- Creating a herb and wildlife garden

- Undertaking a tree planting project

- Undertaking an environmental survey

- Hosting Earth Week

- Raising funds for the Irish Seal Sanctuary

- Marketing paper weights made from aluminium cans, fire blocks from pulped paper and garden containers from waste plastic

- Improving battery recycling in the county

- Promoting home composting.

These projects have the potential to develop an understanding of global issues, but from the information available it is hard to assess whether this is the case. There is some indication that some have a European dimension.

Local authority support

Local Agenda 21 guidance provides an example of government encouragement of local authority support for global education activities, with a focus on sustainable development. *Towards Sustainable Local Communities: guidelines on Local Agenda 21* (Department of Environment and Local Government, 2001) updates the Local Agenda 21 guidelines that were published in 1995. The main focus of Local Agenda 21 is to encourage greater local owner-ship of and participation in decision-making for sustainable develop-ment. The guidance makes suggestions and recommendations which local authorities are encouraged to adopt, including recommenda-tions and ideas for education and schools. One international initia-tive promoted in these guidelines is the Environmental Achievement Awards programme.

Our respondents suggested that there is little or no local authority support for global education in Ireland. No examples of local authority policies or guidelines were identified although, as one res-pondent pointed out, recent initiatives in relation to local authorities targeting 0.7 per cent of their own budgets for overseas aid may benefit global education in the future.

Global education in the school curriculum
Global education is found in both the revised primary curriculum and in the secondary curriculum. While there is an expectation that a cross-curricular approach will be adopted in covering a wide range of issues relevant to global education, there are also specific areas of the school curriculum which focus on aspects of global education.

In the primary curriculum specific aspects of global education are covered in Social Personal and Health Education (SPHE). Three of the specific aims of this subject area are:

- To foster an appreciation of the dignity of every human being

- To develop a sense of social responsibility, a commitment to active and participative citizenship and an appreciation of the democratic way of life

- To enable a child to respect human and cultural diversity and appreciate and understand the interdependent nature of the world (Ruane et al., 1999).

This curriculum is built around three main strands: myself; myself and others; myself and the wider world. Each strand is sub-divided into a number of units, such as: my friends and other people; relating to others; developing citizenship; and media education. These units allow the exploration of a wide range of concepts including culture, identity, friendships, bullying, rights and responsibilities, conflict resolution and respecting difference (Gill *et al.*, 1999). Human rights education is both an explicit and implicit part of SPHE (Ruane *et al.*, 1999).

Strands across other subject areas clearly create opportunities for a global education component. One of the four strands in the science curriculum is that of 'environment awareness and care', while in geography, units within various strands include 'living in the local community'; 'people and places in other areas'; and 'the local natural environment'. Ruane *et al.* (1999) explores how development education can be incorporated into each subject area of the revised primary curriculum and gives examples of themes and topics and a case study of a whole school scheme. The availability of resources that support teachers in incorporating global education across all subject areas in the primary curriculum (for example Gill *et al.*, 1999; NCDE 1999; Ruane *et al.*, 1999) suggests this is a realisable goal.

At the compulsory secondary level (12-15 years), global education features, in particular, in Civic, Social and Political Education (CSPE). This is a discrete and mandatory subject within the Junior Certificate programme (12-15 year olds) that was phased in during 1996/97 following a three-year pilot project. Civics courses traditionally emphasised duty, responsibility and knowledge about specific topics, structures and institutions. Now, much more emphasis is placed on active, participatory citizenship – that is, education *through* citizenship rather than teaching *about* citizenship (Hammond *et al.*, 2001). The current CPSE programme aims to provide students with a dedicated focus on various aspects of citizenship with particular emphasis on active participation. This course is usually provided in one 45 minute period per week over three years (about 70 hours in total) and the four main units of study are:

• the individual and citizenship
• the community
• the State
• Ireland and the world.

Within these broadly defined units teachers have much scope and flexibility to select and deal with specific issues such as gender equity, racism, interculturalism, work and unemployment, poverty, homelessness and the environment. Over the duration of the course, students undertake at least two class or group action projects. The action projects are based on some form of civic, social or political action in students' schools or communities. These have included activities such as inviting local representatives to the school for a question and answer session, protesting on environmental issues, establishing a student council, and campaigning for greater access for people with physical disabilities (Hammond *et al.*, 2001).

Additional steps that were taken to support the introduction and continuation of this programme include:

* regeneration of the teacher's association for CSPE

* provision of modules on CSPE for teacher trainees in some universities

* offering subsidised post-graduate courses to practising teachers

* the production of a four-page supplement on CSPE topics by a national newspaper

* the production of a wide range of resource materials in co-operation with NGOs.

CPSE is formally examined, with about 40 per cent of the marks derived from examination results and 60 per cent from action projects. Other subject areas in the Junior Certificate programme also incorporate various global education components.

Examples of good practice

Events

There are a significant number of global education related projects and events. These are sponsored and supported by both statutory bodies and NGOs. Examples include:

* National debates organised by Concern WorldWide (NGO)

* Lenten Campaign organised by Trócaire (NGO)

- Anti-Racism Day promoted by NCCRI

- UNESCO Associated Schools Project (ASPnet)

- Environmental Achievement Awards Programme

- One World Week organised by Development Education For Youth (NGO).

One World Week

One World Week is a week of youth-led awareness raising, education and action that takes place throughout Ireland during the third week in November every year. During One World Week youth leaders, community workers, teachers, development workers and young people throughout Ireland learn about local and global justice issues and take action to bring about change. Many groups all over the country do activities from the DEFY One World Week activity pack. Some groups organise public events, quizzes and debates, invite guest speakers or have multicultural evenings while others publicly display the work they have done in preparation for One World Week, or lead other people in a public campaign.

One World Week is co-ordinated by DEFY and has been growing as an annual focus for development education since 1985. In 1999, the North South Centre of the Council of Europe designated the third week in November as Global Education Week and now, schools in many European countries take part in One World Week activities. In 2001 One World Week focused on child labour while in 2000 it focused on a critical analysis of the ways in which the media supports or challenges injustices.

Curriculum Development Unit

The Curriculum Development Unit (CDU), established in 1972 by the City of Dublin VEC, Trinity College and the DES, is based within the Education Department of Mary Immaculate College of Education in Dublin. It is a curriculum research and development institute whose work has played a significant role in the promotion of education for democratic citizenship and human rights education. The CDU has produced some excellent classroom resources as well as supported some specific projects. As the examples below indicate, CDU has developed a range of partnerships, bringing together official government bodies and NGOs.

Projects initiated and managed by the Curriculum Development Unit (CDU) for 2000-2001 include:

• Human Rights Education Project

• Human Rights, Conflict and Dialogue Project

• Intercultural Education

• Education for Reconciliation.

Human Rights Education Project
This project, which is sponsored by Trócaire, is now entering its second phase. CDU has worked with key partners to develop a co-ordinated response to the inclusion of Civic, Social and Political Education (CSPE) in the curriculum, delivering in-service training on human rights education to networks of CSPE teachers, and undertaking research on human rights and citizenship education for 15-18 year olds. The project also organises an annual human rights education conference in partnership with Trócaire and Amnesty International.

The Human Rights, Conflict and Dialogue Project
This is an innovative project which links schools in the Republic with schools in Northern Ireland and in Kenya. It is a joint initiative by CDU and the North Eastern and Western Education and Library Boards in Northern Ireland. Trócaire supports the work with Kenya. The project offered students the opportunity to explore key human rights concepts within a classroom setting. Students also undertook an action project on human rights conflict within a local, national or global setting.

Intercultural Education
This project is sponsored by the National Committee for Development Education (NCDE), NCCRI and the DES. The main aim has been to develop training and support materials on intercultural education for teachers of Civic, Social and Political Education (CSPE). In 2000-2001 a group of 12 CSPE teachers from Cork,

Galway and Limerick worked together to develop and pilot materials on intercultural education for the CSPE course.

Initial teacher training

At a formal policy level, there appears to be little in the way of guidance in relation to the various components of global education in initial teacher training. However, some of our respondents suggested that global education is increasingly becoming a part of pre-service training both at primary and secondary levels. Two examples were provided of current developments in this area. The first is a pilot project funded by the NCDE. The NCDE is working with a group of teacher trainers to provide development education modules to BEd students in all primary teacher-training colleges. For post-primary teacher training, the DES has established an expert committee to which WEBS (a network of NGOs) has made a submission on the importance of educating teachers on issues relating to justice, equality and human rights. The National University of Ireland, Maynooth (Co. Kildare) also receives funding from the NCDE to organise a Development Education week for their students on the Higher Diploma in Education.

GE and the continuing professional development of teachers

In Ireland, primary teachers have the opportunity to attend courses over the summer break. These usually take place immediately after school ends for the summer break or just before the next school year begins and are five days in duration, for which teachers receive three days in lieu later that school year. A wide range of courses are available including development education courses. The courses are optional rather than mandatory but are generally well attended. They are provided by a range of organisations including Education Centres, Development Education Centres and sometimes groups of teachers themselves. All courses must be government approved and are required to include a component that addresses gender issues. At secondary level, courses generally take place during the school term. The In-Career Development Unit (ICDU) within the DES provides many of these.

There are a small number of specific opportunities for in-service training in various aspects of global education. The DES, through the ICDU, and a number of NGOs, Education Centres and universities, working independently or in partnership, are providers of such training. NGOs providing in-service training include Amnesty International, Trócaire, WEBS and the Combat Poverty Agency.

Within the Department of Education and Science, ICDU is responsible for funding the following:

- general in-service education sessions through a newly formed Support Service to help with the introduction of the new primary curriculum

- particular in-service training sessions in the summer months for primary teachers, including weeks organised by Development Education Centres

- support services attached to various curriculum areas at secondary level.

NGO networks and activities
There is a wide range of NGOs working within the broad field of global education, many working in partnership with other organisations as part of a wider network. Our respondents emphasised the importance of these organisations in promoting development education and human rights education.

WEBS is an all-Ireland network of individuals and organisations. They work together to promote and support the integration of education for a more just, equal and sustainable world in the secondary curriculum.

NODE. Network of Grassroots in Development Education is the network of development education groups and centres throughout Ireland. It aims to promote the mainstreaming of development education by providing training and by supporting the development of working groups. One working group, for example, has been producing resources and in-service training to enhance social, political and development education within the Transition Year.

Dóchas is an association representing 26 non-governmental development organisations in Ireland. It is also the national platform of the European Union NGO Liaison Committee. One of its working groups is the Development Education Action Group (DEAG). Dóchas and the DEAG are involved in a range of development education initiatives.

CSPE Ad Hoc Group is a network of organisations and educational bodies committed to the development and sustainability of Civic, Social and Political Education within the curriculum. Participants in this group include NGOs, the Department of Education and Science, the National Council for Curriculum and Assessment and the Association of CSPE teachers.

DEFY. Development Education For Youth is a partnership coalition of Irish NGOs and some 20 youth organisations that promotes and co-ordinates development education in the Irish youth sector. Through development education with young people, it aims to foster solidarity with the developing world and raise public awareness in Ireland about development issues. The organisation is primarily focused on non-formal youth work but works increasingly with teachers, developing educational resources, engaging in youth research regarding young people's attitudes to global issues, co-ordinating activities such as One World Week/Global Education Week and cultivating links with European and Southern partners in development by providing international opportunities for young people and youth workers. DEFY supports youth organisations to establish practical development education programmes and to integrate development education fully into their existing pro-grammes.

DEFY's website (www.defy.ie) provides a number of downloadable resources as well as a 'toolkit' for youth workers who want to intro-duce development education into their programmes. The 'toolkit' introduces the concept of development education and its relevance to youth work before elaborating on how a development education programme might be developed and organised. The ready-to-use resources are game and activity-based and are aimed at provoking thought and action on a range of global education issues.

Trócaire was set up in 1973 by the Catholic Bishops of Ireland to support developing countries and to raise awareness within Ireland of development issues. The organisation supports a wide range of development and human rights projects across Africa, Asia, Eastern Europe, the Middle East, Latin and Central America and informs Irish people about what is happening in these countries and about the ways in which they can provide support. Trócaire produces its own resources for school use (see www.trocaire.ie) and it also supports other educational projects (for example, see the CDU's human rights education project). Its income (around €33 million per annum) is largely generated through public donations and fund-raising. Some additional support is provided by the Government and the European Union.

In November 2000 Trócaire launched a special website dedicated to the global human rights dimensions of the Junior Certificate CSPE course (http://trocairecspe.kerna.ie). This comprehensive site allows teachers and students to engage with global and human rights issues in an interactive way and assists students in taking action for a more just world. The site has different sections for teachers, students and parents. The teachers' section includes lesson plans, student activity sheets, guidelines on appropriate methodologies and links to other relevant resources while the students' site provides access to information, activities, discussion groups and specific projects related to the human rights issues covered in the CSPE curriculum. The parents' site provides information on what the CSPE programme is about and suggestions about how parents can help their children meet the aims of the programme.

Research

The NCDE has an Evaluation and Research Working Group that is responsible for the promotion of research into development education. A first step has been an audit of development education research that has taken place over the last ten years. The resulting document (Gannon, 2000) lists 13 different organisations from which research is available and includes information on 60 different research projects, both published and unpublished and undertaken by both statutory bodies (the NCDE, Irish Commission for Justice and Peace, Network of Curriculum Development Units in Development Education) and NGOs (DEFY, Dóchas, Concern WorldWide, Trócaire, 80/20). The author notes that research on development education, has addressed the following themes:

- attitudes to development and justice issues

- development education and the school curriculum

- evaluation of Development Education

- images of developing countries

- links between development education and other aspects of social justice education

- training.

Research into young people and popular culture (Parkin, 2000) highlights the ways in which television might be used as a development education tool. The project illustrates how development and global issues are reflected in young people's interpretation of televised messages. A survey of Irish public attitudes towards a range of development issues, both local and global, provides base line data for the population as a whole on awareness of these issues and determines the level of public support for development co-operation and aid to developing countries. In particular, it establishes levels of awareness and the attitudes of Irish young people to a range of justice and development issues including perceptions of causes of 'problems' in developing countries.

Figure 5.1 summarises the strengths, weaknesses, opportunities and threats to global education in Ireland as identified by our Irish respondents.

Figure 5.1: Strengths, weaknesses, opportunities, threats (SWOT) to GE in Ireland

Strengths	Weaknesses
Strong tradition of global education in Ireland.	Range of 'educations' e.g. DE, HRE, ESD, all placing pressure on schools.
Interested individuals and active NGO sector.	Lack of mainstream/ government support or a coherent policy/strategy for GE.
Establishment of the National Committee for Development Education.	Lack of a clear conceptual base.
New curriculum initiatives which emphasise active learning and action.	An activist-driven at times anti-theoretical bias.
Greater commitment among NGOs to make their DE work more curriculum centred.	Low status of subject areas like CSPE. Inadequate teacher training provision both pre-service and in-service.
Greater co-operation among NGOs in working strategically in education e.g. joint submissions.	Under-resourcing by the DES.
Range of professional development opportunities for teachers.	

Opportunities	Threats
Greater cultural diversity with Ireland.	Growing racism.
Increased funding.	The danger of GE being reduced to a subject within the curriculum.
National commitment to meeting the UN target of 0.7 per cent GNP as overseas development assistance by 2007 and lobbying to allocate 5 per cent of bilateral aid budget to DE.	Other issues more immediate/urgent e.g. examination system. Development of 'virtual citizens' e.g. over-use of Internet for information rather than formation.
Good communication between government and NGOs.	Apathy among general public to global education and action.
CPD courses required to address gender issues.	
Growth of ICT.	
New emphasis on whole school approaches.	
On-going curriculum review.	

6
The Netherlands

The Netherlands is a decentralised unitary state. With a population approaching 16 million and landmass of just 41,000 square kilometres, the Netherlands is one of the most densely populated but smallest countries in the world. There are three tiers of government (central, provincial and municipal) with many powers devolved to provincial and local level. Politically there has been a strong emphasis on consensus and the Dutch government is always a coalition government.

The Netherlands has a long history as a culturally diverse society and as a country of immigration and relatively few people are solely of Dutch heritage. Labour shortages in the 1960s led to the recruitment of migrant workers but immigration is now more restricted. Over 700,000 people (4.5 per cent) of the population do not have Dutch nationality and are classified as foreign or foreign born. This proportion has remained relatively stable over the last decade but disguises the degree of cultural and ethnic diversity within the Netherlands, since many former migrants have taken Dutch nationality. Ethnic minorities are estimated to form around 12 per cent of the population, with families originating in Surinam, the Caribbean, Indonesia and the former Dutch East Indies. A large proportion of more recent migrants to the Netherlands are from Morocco, Turkey, Germany, United Kingdom and United States (OECD, 2001b).

Research suggests that the Dutch are the strongest supporters within the European Union of policies designed to promote equality of opportunity between different ethnic groups in all areas of social life and to promote understanding of different cultures and lifestyles. They also tend to recognise the opportunities for cultural enrichment offered by a culturally diverse society. The Netherlands has a high proportion of actively tolerant people (31 per cent) and a low proportion of intolerant people (11 per cent). Nevertheless, the survey showed that the population of the Netherlands tends to favour the cultural assimilation of minorities more so than most other Europeans. The feeling is that in order to become fully accepted members of Dutch society, people from minority groups must give up their own culture, particularly such aspects of their religious and cultural beliefs which may be in conflict with Dutch law (Thalhammer *et al.*, 2001). Around two thirds (67 per cent) of Dutch respondents fear that education might suffer if the number of children from minority groups is too high. Nevertheless, as in Denmark, a significant majority (62 per cent) believe that where schools make the necessary efforts, the education of all children can be enriched by the presence of minorities. These findings suggest that school leaders have an important role to play in the development of a successful multicultural society with a global outlook.

The values of liberalism and tolerance have featured strongly in the Dutch way of thinking and upholding human rights is an issue about which most people feel strongly, as is evident from the prominent place given to human rights in Article One of the Dutch constitution:

> All persons in the Netherlands shall be treated equally in equal circumstances. Discrimination on the grounds of religion, belief, political opinion, race or sex or on any other grounds whatsoever shall not be permitted (Netherlands Ministry of Foreign Affairs 1989).

The Netherlands is known as a country of progressive human rights legislation. For example, as of 1 April 2001 the Netherlands became the first country in the world to grant same-sex couples access to full civil marriage. The Dutch public's keen interest in human rights situations in other countries is reflected in the broad support given to human rights organisations such as Amnesty International. Dutch foreign policy also expresses a strong national commitment to human rights. The Netherlands spent 0.79 per cent of its GDP on Overseas Development Aid in 1999, which is the second highest among the case study countries (OECD, 2001b).

Education policy: an overview

In the Netherlands, compulsory education consists of three phases: primary education (ages 5-12); basic secondary education (ages 12-15); and upper secondary education (ages 16-18). Each phase has an outline national curriculum consisting of core curriculum subjects and some general educational objectives. The latter are cross-disciplinary objectives relating to social issues and skills.

There has always been considerable freedom within Dutch education as to who can found a school and to curriculum content, materials, methods and school organisation. One important feature of the Dutch education system is the right of parents to establish a school. Under paragraph 23 of the Constitution parents are guaranteed freedom of denomination and organisation, which means that they may found a school on the basis of religious, philosophical, educational and teaching principles. Consequently, around a third of schools are publicly run and the other two thirds are private schools which, providing they comply with statutory requirements, can claim the same financial support as public schools.

Early Education Acts stipulated that certain subjects were to be taught but there were no statutory requirements with regard to specific content, method or time spent on each subject. While there is still much scope for schools to design and implement their own specific programmes, a set of core objectives for compulsory subjects was introduced by the Government during the 1990s. These provide a general outline of what each school should offer and the minimum levels of student knowledge and skills. The exact way in which these general objectives are to be met, the level that is to be obtained, specific content and the time to be spent on different subjects is not prescribed. Suggestions are made but schools still have much control over the programmes that they provide.

At primary level there are no compulsory national examinations but around 70 per cent of schools use the tests for primary school leavers developed by the National Institute for Educational Measurement (CITO) to assess pupils' level of attainment at the end of primary schooling. These results are used to help determine the most appropriate course of secondary education for each pupil. The different courses for secondary education have common, specialised and optional components but also serve to direct students towards vocational, further or higher education. There are national compulsory examinations for students aged 15 years at the end of basic education. There has been considerable public debate as to whether the results of these examinations should be published, with concern expressed about the ways in which this may promote a publicly competitive spirit between students and schools (Davies and Kirkpatrick, 2000).

Over recent years there has been a trend towards greater autonomy and decentralisation with many central government powers devolved to the individual school or local authority (Karsten, 1998). Under the 1992 Education Participation Act schools are required to have a participation council which includes equal numbers of staff and parent representatives and which is responsible for consulting with the head on school matters. There is no student representation on this council at primary level. At secondary level staff representatives on the participation council are matched by an equal number of 'pupil/ parent' representatives. It is left to school boards to determine the precise means by which learners may participate in school decision-making.

While historically the achievement of minority ethnic students in Dutch schools has tended to be below that of their white peers, progress is now being made. At primary level children with a mother tongue other than Dutch may, if their parents wish, be taught in that language (Eurydice, 2000b). Minorities are achieving at an equivalent level in primary schools; while in secondary education, participation rates are virtually equal to that of their Dutch counterparts. Moroccan and Turkish pupils are, however, far more likely to attend lower-level secondary schools, and are less likely to go on to higher education (Netherlands Ministry of Education, Culture and Science, 1998c).

The importance of supporting schools in familiarising themselves with the cultural and educational backgrounds of minority ethnic pupils, particularly those of Turkish and Moroccan backgrounds, has been prioritised by the Ministry (Netherlands Ministry of Education,

Culture and Science, 1998c). There is also currently a strong emphasis on developing Dutch language competence among immigrant pupils and their families. The focus is on developing better methods for teaching Dutch and on encouraging greater participation of immigrant children in early childhood education. Schools with large numbers of ethnic minority pupils receive additional financial support from the government through a funding formula that counts immigrant children as 1.9 for funding purposes (Netherlands Ministry of Education, Culture and Science, 1998b).

Ministry of Education initiatives

The national curriculum, as set out by the Ministry of Education, makes it clear that schools are required to incorporate aspects of global education into the various subject areas. While there is a requirement to teach certain subjects, the exact content, method or how much time is devoted to particular areas is not prescribed and educational institutes are free to decide how to implement these general guidelines.

Hooghoff (2001) identifies three Ministry of Education policy documents that have promoted 'the global dimension' in Dutch education: *Widening Horizons* (1991); *Unbounded Talent* (1997); and *Unbounded Talent Action Plan* (1998). The latter document focuses specifically on the 'internationalisation' of Dutch education and the ways in which this has been promoted by cross border co-operation with Germany and Belgium by engagement in major European Community programmes such as Socrates and Leonardo. Ministry policy is that activities with an international dimension must become a standard part of the curriculum. The Unbounded Talent Action Plan outlines some of the national programmes that teachers and students can become involved in, largely student and teacher exchanges with other European countries.

The Ministry of Education is responsible for a website (www. kennisnet.nl) which provides teachers and students with information on general international events as well as specific items of interest such as the Climate Conference (2000), World Environment Day (5 June) and International Human Rights Day (10 December). The Centre for Global Education (CMO), a non-governmental organisation, is funded by the Ministry to produce around 40 sets of teaching materials each year for this website.

The Ministry also finances the *Europees Platform* (www.europee splatform.nl) which was set up to strengthen the European dimension in education and promote internationalisation. This body is responsible for informing Dutch schools about resources and programmes that involve co-operation with other European countries. It also administers a national programmes fund to which schools can apply to establish and run partnerships with schools in other countries. There is particular emphasis on co-operation with Belgium and Germany, which border directly on the Netherlands.

Through the Directorate of ICT and Internationalisation, the Ministry supports schools and institutes to participate in European networks such European Schoolnet (www.eun.org) and UNESCO's Associated Schools Project (ASPnet).

Another Ministry document, *Knowledge: give and take- internationalisation of education in the Netherlands* (2000), outlines the agreements between the Ministry for Development Co-operation and the Ministry of Education for educational co-operation through the extension of the CENESA (Co-operation in Education between the Netherlands and South Africa) programme. Nevertheless, these initiatives do not promote global education in its broadest sense, with most focusing on European rather than broader international co-operation. They do not appear to be widely distributed or known about among non-governmental organisations concerned with global education.

Other Ministry initiatives
The Ministry for Development Co-operation produces its own educational materials and also funds the National Committee for International Co-operation and Sustainable Development (NCDO). The NCDO receives a budget for promoting activities in the Netherlands on subjects related to international development. Part of this budget is allocated for educational activities. Most of this fund is allocated to organisations such as the Centre for Global Education (CMO) that develop specific school projects.

CMO is an independent institute that specialises in the documentation, analysis and production of a wide range of educational materials relevant to global education. Information on over 7,500 educational resources is available on a searchable database. Specific resources produced by the institute include essay packs for 10-15 year olds covering 75 different Global Education topics and CD-ROMS on sustainable development for 16-18 year olds. CMO also produces *Per Expresse*, the Dutch variant of Global Express and a variety of teaching packs for schools.

Several Ministries cooperate in the inter-departmental project Learning for Sustainability. This project aims to promote, among other things, the implementation of education for sustainable development. NCDO is one of the co-ordinating institutes and two projects being financed under this initiative are DOOR! and GLOBE. DOOR! aims to support teachers to develop their own programmes of education for sustainability. GLOBE is an internet project in which schools all over the world participate in active learning about the environment.

The International Institute for Communication and Development (IICD) was established as an independent foundation by the Netherlands Ministry for Development Co-operation in 1997. It aims to assist developing countries to utilise the opportunities offered by information and communication technologies towards realising sustainable development. There are currently eight participating developing countries (Bolivia, Burkina Faso, Ghana, Jamaica, Mali, Tanzania, Uganda, Zambia). The organisation supports and promotes a number of projects relating to good governance, education, health and environment. Information on two education projects (Global Teenager and Adopt-a-School) is given later in this case study.

The Anne Frank House, which is an independent non-profit organisation, provides public education related to the Holocaust and to anti-discrimination more broadly. Its main activities centre on the Anne Frank House museum, international travelling exhibitions and a library and documentation centre. It is funded by government and by museum fees. The travelling exhibitions aim to stimulate thinking about the importance of tolerance, human rights and democracy and to encourage people to identify similarities and differences between events during World War II and today. Additional teaching material accompanies the exhibition, including an educational pack for teachers who are encouraged to work on the various themes in school before and after their visit. Anne Frank House also acts as the national contact point for the European Information Network on Racism and Xenophobia (RAXEN) established in 2001.

Response to international initiatives

As reported above, there is some encouragement by the Ministry of Education for school involvement in international initiatives but from the information available it is difficult to assess the extent of this in comparison with the other case study countries. Of those examples found, all of them made extensive use of the internet.

GLOBE (Global Learning and Observations to Benefit the Environment)

GLOBE is a US co-ordinated, worldwide, hands-on, primary and secondary school-based science and education programme. There are currently over one million pupils in more than 10,000 schools across 96 countries that take part in the programme. The activities for this project occur across different curriculum areas including: physics, chemistry, biology, geography, foreign languages, ICT, agriculture. One of the main activities GLOBE students are involved in is taking scientifically valid measurements of the atmosphere, water and soil. They use the internet to report these to the student data archive. Both the collection and analysis of data provide opportunities for collaboration with scientists and other GLOBE students around the world.

The Netherlands joined GLOBE in 1995 and around 120 secondary schools are currently involved in the project. This represents approximately 15 per cent of all Dutch secondary schools although not all these schools are active members. Within the Netherlands, the project is funded by five different Ministries (Environment, Education, Agriculture, Traffic, Foreign Affairs). GLOBE Netherlands provides schools with information on schools in other countries that want to collaborate with Dutch schools. There is also some collaboration between GLOBE Germany, GLOBE Switzerland and GLOBE Netherlands to develop a joint Rhine-project.

Other than the environmental data collection and reporting, there is a range of other national and international activities that GLOBE students can become involved in. Examples include:

- As part of the Dutch Science and Technology week, GLOBE students were invited to design a poster expressing the need for international environmental co-operation and the contributions made by the GLOBE programme

- Along with five other countries and in collaboration with a Dutch initiative to work on CO2 management (United Air Fund), Dutch students contributed poems and essays to a book on the importance of clean air

- Students from one participating school in the Netherlands served as ambassadors for the GLOBE programme. In March 2000 they attended a meeting of the World Water Forum (an international body of professionals devoted to the preservation and enhancement of global water) and shared GLOBE's contributions to monitoring the world's water environments.

Government financial support for GLOBE is likely to be reduced in the future and so there are moves to establish greater participation and support from the private and local government sectors. In particular, partnerships are being sought with scientific institutions, universities, local authorities and senior (elderly) volunteers.

Local authority support

Across the Netherlands it appears that there is wide variation in the levels of local authority support for global education initiatives. Although many municipalities have links with municipalities abroad and some local authorities integrate global education into their policies, this is by no means universal. Nevertheless, Learning for Sustainability, the inter-departmental Government initiative detailed earlier, occurs in each of the twelve provinces in the Netherlands. Each province is responsible for organising a range of activities, including activities within education. Both primary and secondary schools play an active role in this project.

GE in the school curriculum

Individual schools and teachers have considerable freedom to determine their own priorities in relation to global education and to put a greater (or lesser) emphasis on the different aspects of global education. Some schools have developed strong antiracist policies while others will have focused on particular North-South projects or on other human rights issues.

Various aspects of global education are incorporated into mandatory core objectives and attainment targets at all three levels of compulsory education. They are usually covered in the form of cross-curricular themes. The core objectives describe the minimum levels of pupils' knowledge and skills and provide a basic framework rather than specifying to what level or how these objectives are to be met.

Revised core objectives for primary education (age 4-12) came into force in 1998 and are outlined in *Primary Education in the Netherlands* (Boland, 1999). There are two types of core objectives (cross-curricular objectives and subject specific objectives) both of which include elements of global education. Many of these elements (for example citizenship, developing countries, environmental education, European dimensions and intercultural education) come into the subject specific curriculum area 'orientation on man and the world'. This curriculum area includes geography, history, society, technology, the environment and nature study.

Basic secondary education provides a broad and general education for all students aged between 12 and 15 years. In August 1993, a new curriculum was introduced consisting of six general attainment targets and targets for each of the 15 compulsory subjects. Clear elements of global education can be found in both sets of targets. The most explicit example is found in 'cross-disciplinary themes' which states that attention should be paid to:

• recognising and dealing with one's own standards and values and those of other people

• recognising and dealing with the similarities and differences between the sexes

- the relationship between mankind and nature and the concept of sustainable development

- active citizenship in a democratic and multicultural society and in the international community (Netherlands Ministry of Education, Culture and Science, 1998b: 11, 1.1 -1.4)

With regard to the latter, each specific subject area is divided into a number of 'fields', many of which include aspects of global education. Multicultural society, nature and the environment and international developments contain such elements.

In geography for example, target 4 states:

Pupils should be able to explain the significance in relation to their daily lives of geographical issues, in particular, issues connected with ... ethnic segregation and/or integration, the environment and sustainable development, European integration, the global development question and development co-operation (Netherlands Ministry of Education, Culture and Science, 1998b: 32)

In history, target 8 states:

By reference to examples from the Netherlands in the seventeenth century and in the early industrial periods, pupils should be able to recognise how the social positions of individuals and groups are (partly) determined by factors such as origin, ethnicity, religion, wealth, education and gender (Netherlands Ministry of Education, Culture and Science, 1998b: 39)

In physics and chemistry, target 20 states:

With regard to the use of water, detergents, cosmetics, energy and sound, pupils should be able to relate what they have learned to nature, the environment and sustainable development (Netherlands Ministry of Education, Culture and Science, 1998b: 67)

The courses available at upper secondary level (age 15-18) lead up to national and school-based examinations. These programmes consist of general skills, subject specific skills and subject specific content and also contain elements of global education. Civics is a mandatory programme at this level. One example of a newly developed programme combining history and civics consists of five domains:

- skills and approaches
- constitutional state
- parliamentary democracy
- welfare state
- multicultural society.

Within these domains, the meaning and history of each concept, the values underpinning historical and current practices, and the rights and obligations of freedom are explored.

Hooghoff (2001) notes that since the 1970s, schools have been expected to pay attention to international issues such as developing countries, human rights and environmental issues. Despite this, one of our respondents was of the view that citizenship education is not strongly prioritised in Dutch education. He suggested that history is the only subject in basic education where civics in the narrow sense is covered systematically and that citizenship education in the broader sense, including aspects such as preparation for active participative citizenship in a global multicultural society, remains somewhat marginalised. This view is broadly supported by Hahn (1999) who carried out a study of citizenship education in Dutch schools during the mid-1990s. She confirms that although *maatschappijleer* or 'study of society' is incorporated into the study of history, genuine citizenship learning which addresses skills and which will enable democratic participation depend on the interests of the individual teacher:

> Dutch students in my sample were less likely than students in the other countries [Denmark, England, Germany, USA] to be asked to express their views on contentious public policy issues that they had investigated. But in the Netherlands, it is not expected that schools have a particular role to play in preparing students for democratic debate and decision-making (Hahn, 1999: 238-9).

There is little explicit reference to human rights education in the national curriculum, which contrasts with the relatively high profile of human rights issues in government, the media and business. Nevertheless, education as a whole successfully reflects many human rights concepts and there is potential to develop these within the curriculum. Much would seem to depend on the interests and skills of individual teachers.

Examples of good practice

Schools appear to be involved in a wide range of global education projects supported to a large degree by various NGOs. Examples include:

The Global Teenager Project

Global Teenager is an international network of secondary school students. The project is supported by the IICD (International Institute for Communication and Development) and began with a pilot study in 1999 where students in schools in the Netherlands and South Africa participated in a series of virtual discussions. The pilot study subsequently developed into the Global Teenager Project which aims to create a safe and controlled space for students and teachers to discover and practice international learning. Using the internet, subjects are discussed and experiences shared. There are currently some 75 schools and around 2000 students from ten different countries (both developed and developing) that are actively participating in this network.

Adopt-a-School is another IICD supported project in which organisations and companies are offered the opportunity to adopt a school in a developing country. Using the internet, students communicate with each other and learn from and about one another's lifestyles.

Zimsurf is an interactive web-based education programme for secondary schools in the Netherlands that has been developed by LSO and is supported by the City-Link Haarlem-Mutare Foundation. The programme has a strong international focus but has been designed to fit the course and targets for geography and economics students. It meets educational goals for both ICT and global education (see www.zimsurf.nl).

Per Expresse is the Dutch version of 'Global Express', an interactive quarterly 'for those who care about the future'. It aims to provide an alternative to mass media and student publications and is circulated to regional contacts in over 15 countries. In the Netherlands this project is supported by CMO and includes a teaching pack as well as a range of global education related information for teachers and students.

The City-Link Haarlem-Mutare Foundation organises the official city-link between Haarlem (Netherlands) and Mutare (Zimbabwe). The foundation organises activities aimed at engaging people in world development issues generally and in those of Mutare, Zimbabwe in particular. City councils as well as a variety of organisations participate in the activities. A range of educational resources and projects for both primary and secondary level are available.

A Journey to Mutare (Zimbabwe)

This project is designed to last about two weeks and focuses on various aspects of life in the city of Mutare. It includes a teaching package with audio-visual material and an exhibition about children in Mutare. The resource caters for lower, middle and upper school pupils. The aim is that by concentrating on one city, pupils get an idea of everyday life there. Connections are also made with care of the environment and recycling of materials. There are workshops in African music and dance, conducted by African teachers and the project concludes with a festive evening to which parents are invited. Approximately 25 Haarlem schools have participated in the project since it began in 1994 and there are generally more applications for the project than the City-Link can provide for.

Titambira mu Zimababwe (Welcome to Zimbabwe)

This project aims to provide students with insights and knowledge about Zimbabwe by involving them in conducting independent surveys. Some of the focus themes include: tourism, water problems for agriculture, and everyday life and culture. The package includes a teachers' guide, pupil booklets, slides, information about the themes, a videotape and photographic materials.

This is a journey

This series of lessons, developed by LSO, has an international focus (Indonesia, Surinam, Zimbabwe) and is designed to meet objectives of the core curriculum across a number of subject areas including economics, history, geography and care. The materials are kept in a suitcase that travels with the students from one lesson to another. It is also now available as an ICT project.

Centres for International Co-operation
There are 16 Centres for International Co-operation across the Netherlands that give teachers access to global education resources. Schools are also informed by direct mail, national educational exhibitions and websites. For example, www.unhchr.ch/hredu.nsf is a database of human rights education programmes and resources.

Initial teacher training and the continuing professional development of teachers

Teacher training is usually four years in duration for both primary and secondary schools, although some secondary teachers complete a one-year postgraduate programme. Primary teachers receive general training and are expected to teach all subjects. Secondary teachers specialise and many have a university degree in the subject they teach.

In 1996 the Minister established a programme for the improvement of teacher education colleges. The main aims were the establishment of a joint curriculum for teacher education colleges, greater regional collaboration between teacher education institutes and professional development of teacher educators (Koster and Snoek, 1998).

As far as our respondents were aware, there are no guidelines or legislation in relation to global education and the training of teachers. Similarly, the opportunities for in-service training in relation to global education were viewed as limited. One respondent noted that the opportunities that do exist are optional rather than mandatory. The DOOR! project, cited earlier, is one opportunity that teachers have to participate in in-service training about global sustainability.

NGO networks and activities

Respondents noted that many NGOs are involved in training, developing materials, advising schools, and organising special projects. Examples provided include:

- Institute for Public Politics (IPP)
- Centres for International Co-operation
- Institute for Nature and Environmental Education in Amsterdam
- International Institute for Communication and Development (IICD)

- City-Link Haarlem-Mutare Foundation
- National Agency for Global Education (LSO)
- Platform Mensenrechten-educatie (Human Rights Education).

The Platform on Human Rights Education was established in the Netherlands in 1996. The secretariat of this platform is the Netherlands' Commission for UNESCO whose mandate in relation to human rights education is to support, stimulate and co-ordinate activities within education as well as to provide information to Dutch professionals in education. Examples of participating organisations include:

- Amnesty International
- Anne Frank Foundation
- 4 and 5 May Committee, Dutch Red Cross
- Dutch UNICEF Foundation
- Centre for Global Education (CMO)
- Dutch Foundation for Curriculum Development.

FORUM, the Institute for Multicultural Development, is a national centre of expertise in multicultural development and provides an example of co-operation between the Dutch government and minority groups. The organisation's remit is to promote the interests and effective integration of minority groups in Dutch society which it achieves primarily through its project and research work. FORUM acts in an advisory capacity to government departments and NGOs and is also active in the areas of housing, employment, education, health care, art and culture, and political participation. This work is supported by subsidies from the Ministry of Health, Welfare and Sport.

One educational project organised by FORUM is *Minority Youth Promotion Teams* which aim to encourage more minority youth to enter higher education by providing role models in secondary schools. Team members also work with potential employers to eliminate misconceptions about minorities looking for work. FORUM has also produced training material for teachers involved in 'newcomer education' and has held conferences and debates on the education and integration of minority students.

Research and publications

The NCDO and SLO have undertaken research in the area of global education. One example cited was *Human Rights through the Curriculum* (Bron, 2001). *Developing a Global Dimension in Dutch Education* (Hooghoff, 2001) provides a useful analysis of past and current developments in the Netherlands relating to 'internationalisation'.

Figure 6.1 summarises the strengths, weaknesses, opportunities and threats to global education in the Netherlands, as identified by our Dutch respondents.

Figure 6.1: Strengths, weaknesses, opportunities, threats to GE in the Netherlands (SWOT)

Strengths	Weakness
Cross-curricular work broadens pupils' knowledge and understanding of global issues.	Cross-curricular work and no formal examination means GE may not be taken as seriously as it should.
Some funds are available to support NGO initiatives.	Good ideas are turned down because of limited financial resources and narrow funding criteria.
Existence of good materials and resources to support GE work.	Schools have limited knowledge about the resources that are available or there are limited funds available to get them into schools.
	Limited training opportunities for teachers.

Opportunities	Threats
GE is not only about themes (content) but is also about pedagogy. Both of these aspects provide opportunities for success.	The current situation in the Dutch schools: changing programmes, lack of materials, equipment, time and teachers.
Co-operation between public and private sectors.	
The use of ICT.	
International, social and economic developments.	

7

Global education and
citizenship education

In each of the four case study countries global education is recognised as being of importance and is supported by broad policy statements at central government level. Each country acknowledges the need to educate its citizens to live together in an interdependent world and makes provision for some form of social and political education, whether or not the term citizenship education is used. This chapter builds on the case studies to explore how citizenship education might act as a vehicle for global education, or education which enables young people to be active cosmopolitan citizens, working to promote democracy, development and human rights.

Strengths and limitations of current policy frameworks

Generally speaking, ministries of education recognise the importance of some form of global education, particularly within the compulsory years of schooling. They acknowledge, implicitly or explicitly, the economic effects of globalisation and the importance of economic competitiveness within this context. Although governments recognise a role for global education, it is rarely a funding priority within the ministry of education. It is normally the ministry of foreign affairs/international development which takes a lead in supporting educational initiatives to promote international development and solidarity with the poorest countries of the world. While such programmes may explore questions of global interdependence, they are less likely to tackle questions of human rights and social justice at home.

There is considerable variation across the four case study countries in the specificity of guidance provided by central government. In Denmark, and to a lesser degree in the Netherlands, for example, individual schools have considerable freedom to define content and the extent to which global dimensions will be incorporated into school programmes. In all four countries there appears to be little consideration of how international initiatives and recommendations, such as those of the Council of Europe, are communicated by national governments to schools, local authorities and other interested parties.

With the possible exception of the Netherlands, local authority support for global education in the case study countries appears to be weak. While there are policy documents at local or regional level, these are not always translated into concrete actions. Where we have examples of local authorities taking a lead in developing specific policies or actions, such as the Learning for Sustainability initiative in the Netherlands or multicultural and antiracist policies in certain English local authorities, then developments at local authority level can be particularly effective and influential. This is most likely if they are carried out in co-operation with local communities and NGOs.

NGOs are most effective in providing support for global education where they have the benefit of a national platform or umbrella group. In particular, this enables them to lobby national governments and to establish effective working relationships and potential partnerships with government departments. However, where umbrella groups do exist, they appear to have given greater emphasis to particular aspects of global education, so that development education, environmental education, and education for sustainable development seem to have been prioritised at the expense of other aspects of global education, such as human rights and intercultural education. The most significant contribution of NGOs appears to be in providing teaching materials and packs and, most recently, web-based resources to support global education, particularly in the formal, school sector. There is, however, little evaluation of the impact of this work.

The teacher-training curriculum does not appear to have kept pace with the demands of the school curriculum in relation to global education. In all four countries, respondents recognised the importance of including global dimensions into initial teacher training. However, with the exception of Denmark, where the Teacher Training Act 1998 specifies that international themes must be part of teacher training, there appears to be little guidance at formal policy level in relation to global education in initial teacher training.

The in-service training and professional development of teachers is another area which has been largely neglected with respect to global education. There appear to be no mandatory requirements in any of the four countries surveyed. The availability of courses specialising in aspects of global education and the extent to which these opportunities are taken up varied considerably across the four countries. For example, it appears that Irish teachers enjoy a range of courses, supported by universities and training institutions working in partnership with NGOs. The school year is structured so as to allow for primary school teachers to engage in training at a particular time, rather than to complete it in their own time. In other countries, the take-up of such courses is relatively low. This low take-up is explained in terms of competing curriculum pressures on teachers.

The internet is increasingly being used for accessing and sharing information, communicating with others across the world and for taking part in international global education initiatives. There is a range of web-based resources and interactive websites to support learning and teaching. School linking is seen as an important aspect of global education.

A strong theme across the four countries is the growing interest in international development and global dimensions in education. An area appearing to need further development is intercultural and anti-racist work. All four countries are culturally diverse, yet there appears to be a neglect of questions of equality in contexts of diversity and of human rights and social justice issues as they relate to the communities in which learners live. In all four countries there appears to be a preference for addressing international issues, and a tendency to overlook parallel issues in local communities. Current programmes and initiatives do not necessarily make explicit the connections between local, national and global concerns.

Our survey suggests that this area of education is under-researched. Information about research came mainly from academics; practitioners, the potential users of the research, were not necessarily aware of it. There is an urgent need for both NGOs and academics to initiate dialogue. Researchers and research organisations need to ensure that their work is accessible and applicable. NGOs and other practitioners need to acquaint themselves with the research, consider its significance and be willing to engage more readily in on-going critical processes of self-evaluation. In particular, those offering training or producing resources and other materials need to recognise the need for accountability and project evaluation, including self-evaluation.

Citizenship and belonging in Britain

We have suggested, in chapter two, that since citizenship education is given increasing importance in a range of countries world-wide, it provides a means by which global education can be mainstreamed. In other words, citizenship education offers a specific focus for initiatives which promote democracy, development and human rights. At the same time, if global education is to be mainstreamed, we need to ensure that its aims and objectives permeate the whole of the school curriculum, both the taught curriculum and the informal curriculum. Global education is unlikely to be successful if it is restricted to lessons entitled Citizenship.

In order to consider whether, and how, citizenship education might play a role in mainstreaming global education in England, we need to reflect first on the nature of citizenship itself. Although there have been extensive debates about the nature of citizenship and identity in Britain, as a result of constitutional reform, these debates appear to touch some sectors of the population more sharply than others. Until relatively recently, English identity was not subject to close scrutiny, and was often confused with British identity. Debates about the development of a multicultural society have tended to focus on visible minority groups, notably those whose families originate in the Indian sub-continent or the Caribbean. The identities of these citizens, and the degree to which they feel part of the wider society, continue to attract considerable media commentary. In order to understand these debates they need to be seen within their historical context.

In the mid-twentieth century, immigration from the Caribbean and from the Indian sub-continent was recognised as a useful solution to labour shortages, but from the 1960s onwards immigration controls on Commonwealth settlers, passed to appease racist opinion, served to undermine black settlers by institutionalising racism and equating such settlers with the status of 'undesirable immigrant'. This effectively relegated a whole category of British people to second class citizenship (Fryer, 1984). E.R. Braithwaite, the author of the novel *To Sir, With Love*, summed it up as follows:

> In spite of my years of residence in Britain, any service I might render the community in times of war or peace, any contribution I might make or wish to make, or any feeling of identity I might entertain towards Britain and the British, I – like all other colored persons in Britain – am considered an 'immigrant'. Although this term indicates that we have secured entry into Britain, it describes a continuing condition in which we have no real hope of ever enjoying the desired transition to full responsible citizenship (Braithwaite, 1967, quoted in Fryer, 1984: 382).

Braithwaite's observation that 'full responsible citizenship' was denied black settlers, however much they identified with Britain and wished to belong, still has some resonance today for particular minority groups. Many British citizens continue to be viewed as outsiders, as can be observed in more recent debates about the allegiance of British Muslims (Richardson, 1997). All young people, including those from minority communities, are likely to have multiple identities. Our research with young people in Leicester suggests that young people recognise the ways in which they are being labelled by others but do not let this dominate their sense of self. These quotations indicate they are only too aware of how the wider society defines their communities and how public discourse serves to label those seen as 'other'. Nevertheless these young people wish to be accepted on their own terms:

> I am a Hindu and most would consider me to be of Indian origin as my parents came from there. I consider myself to be British as I was born and brought up here. *Anjali*

> Ireland plays a part in my life. I'm open to all, not part of anything, preferring to decide for myself what I believe rather than take on one particular belief. *Sean*

> First and foremost I am a Muslim. I am a British Muslim, but really our culture is known as an Asian culture. *Mohammed*

> I'm White, English. I hate the idea of small white village communities which are very parochial. I hate people using words like 'half caste' or 'coloured'. *David* (from Osler and Starkey, 2002, forthcoming).

The degree to which these young people have a sense of belonging to their town and to their local communities is particularly strong. For many, a sense of Britishness, of belonging to the nation, came, in part, from a need to assert British identity in the face of an externally imposed identity – *'most would consider me to be of Indian origin ... I consider myself to be British'*. All were able to look critically at their own cultural and family contexts and see how their own identities differed from those of their parents or grandparents. Many were able to look beyond their local identity to international communities or reference points, whether defined by religion, culture, parents' country of origin or family migration. In this sense, all had attitudes and experiences which might be considered assets in the building of a cosmopolitan citizenship.

We have argued that an inclusive concept of citizenship needs also to recognise diversity within white populations and to be built upon a vision of multiculturalism which is inclusive of white communities (Osler, 1999 and 2001). It is critical that white citizens also feel a sense of belonging and are able to sign up to this ideal. One commentator has suggested that:

> The problem is not that ethnic minorities are alienated from a concept of Britishness but that there is today no source of Britishness from which anyone – black or white – can draw inspiration (Malik, 2002).

Malik's provocative claim may partially be explained by the ways in which understandings of national identity, like so much in Britain, are implicit, rather than explicit. It may also be somewhat one-sided, since there are many things, including sporting achievements, aspects of the natural environment, architectural heritage and historical monuments, of which Britons of different backgrounds may be proud. Malik's claim may, however, relate to the period of history in which we find ourselves. At the mid-point of the twentieth century, Britain still represented the centre of an empire, many of whose subjects saw themselves as British. Within Britain, children were taught to be proud of their country's past and present achievements. During the second half of the twentieth century, however, not only did that empire collapse, but many British people became aware of its limitations and of shameful aspects of colonial rule. During the same period, many settlers arriving in the 'mother country' found that, although they had British citizenship, they were seen in Britain as 'not quite British'. History today is less likely to be taught as a series of great achievements but presented in its complexity, from a range of different perspectives. Citizens can no longer draw uncritical inspiration from their country's past glories, but are expected to face up to a more complex reality. Thus, some citizens have struggled to find something new to which they can belong, whereas others have been reminded that they do not quite belong. There are now many ways of being British, although they may not all be equally valued. We have reached a point where a new and inclusive national identity based on a common sense of belonging is required:

> Many Britons feel that everybody's culture is celebrated but their own. The multiculturalism debate has not recognised the many ways in which the various political and cultural anxieties of whites and non-whites are similar and inextricably linked (Alibhai Brown, 2000).

The degree to which newcomers to Britain can ever be truly British has been brought into question again in the months following the terrorist attacks of 11 September 2001. In December 2001 Home Secretary David Blunkett proposed that immigrants who had settled in Britain should be required to demonstrate a 'modest grasp' of English and a simple test of their understanding of British democracy and culture (*The Guardian*, 10 December 2001: 1). These comments came in the wake of concerns about riots in Bradford, Burnley and Oldham in summer 2001, in which the far right British National Party was implicated. The labelling of the violence and conflict as a race riot reinforces the somewhat simplistic notion that the problem is the minority community which refuses to integrate and belong. This is despite evidence that these riots in a number of Northern English towns had been provoked by a racist political party which sought to exploit distrust, political alienation and a sense of injustice felt by many white residents.

A Home Office commissioned report into the riots noted the segregation of communities in these towns, including the educational segregation created by the selection procedures of church schools (Cantle, 2001). An independent report into the Oldham riots criticised the 'self-segregation' of minority communities and the failure of minority leaders to encourage integration (Richie, 2001). The Home Secretary's remarks on citizenship have since been developed into proposals, outlined in the nationality, immigration and asylum White Paper *Secure Borders, Safe Haven* (Home Office, 2002) that those applying for British nationality should be required to pass English language and citizenship tests and to undergo a simple ceremony in which they swear an oath of allegiance. As the Home Secretary explained:

> To welcome others who need our protection or have a contribution to make to our society, we must be secure within a shared sense of belonging and identity. Strong civic and community foundations are necessary if we are to secure integration with diversity. They will enable us to reach out and embrace those who seek to make our country their home, to work, to contribute or to escape from persecution, torture or death (Home Office, 7 February 2002 – press release).

The Home Secretary is right to define ' a shared sense of belonging and identity' as a prerequisite for citizenship, but that sense of belonging is not easily achieved in a society in which racism remains a barrier to full participation and citizenship. Strong civic and community foundations may be necessary, but if all are to be accepted as of equal worth then all citizens need to acquire skills of intercultural communication and evaluation, as discussed here in chapter two.

The Home Secretary's concerns appear, first, to centre on a fear that diversity is, in itself, a problem. Certainly, the Government suggests that the number of people applying for asylum in the UK is too high. While significant numbers of asylum seekers present an administrative challenge, and any government may wish to provide alternative entry procedures for asylum-seekers and other migrants, this argument echoes the arguments of previous decades, that the number of migrants is, in itself, a problem. Since the 1960s governments have argued that 'too many' migrants, however defined, threaten good race relations (Dummett, 1973; Osler, 1997a). For example, in 1991, the then Foreign Secretary Douglas Hurd told Amnesty International that although he 'understood and shared Amnesty's concern' to ensure that 'Britain respects its obligations to the refugee', this had to be reconciled 'with a truth dinned into me through the years when I was Home Secretary, namely that the good race relations between communities in this country depend to a very large extent on a firm and fair system of immigration control' (*The Guardian*, 26 November 1991). This type of argument seems to have prevailed both in periods of high unemployment and when there have been labour shortages.

Secondly, Home Secretary David Blunkett's statement seems to imply that some groups may have voluntarily opted out of their civic responsibilities and sense of belonging. There is little acknowledgement that, for many, the barriers to belonging are substantial.

The Cantle Report (2001), which sought to establish why there were riots in the spring and summer of 2001, suggested that a national debate was needed to establish a new understanding and new agreed values between all sections of the community:

> we would expect the new values to contain statements about the expectation that the use of English language, which is a pre-condition of citizenship, (or a commitment to become fluent within a period of time) will become more rigorously pursued, with appropriate support (Cantle, 2001: 19: 5.1.11)

The suggestion that all settlers in Britain need to speak English and the suggestion that a lack of competence in English language is a factor in the breakdown of community cohesion overlooks the fact that many of the young people who engaged in rioting were bi-lingual. Limited understanding of English may have contributed to the segregation of some of their parents and grandparents, but not to theirs. They speak English in certain contexts, for example, to their teachers. In other contexts, for example, in conversation with their elders, they use a community language. It is of concern that some politicians have seen their bilingualism, not as an asset, but as symbolic of disaffection or not belonging. Although language can act as a barrier to exclude and the ability to communicate in English is likely to be a key element in economic and political inclusion, there are other sources of political disaffection, the roots of which lie in poverty and unemployment. These barriers need to be addressed at the same time as that of racism. All continue to exclude some groups from full participation and citizenship.

A further concern is the Home Secretary's distinction between those new settlers that are coming to work and 'to contribute' and those who are coming to escape from persecution torture or death. This is to ignore the fact that throughout history, refugee communities have made a substantial contribution to the country. In other words, in the UK, where there is a lower acceptance of refugees and asylum seekers than in many other states across Europe (Thalhammer *et al.*, 2001), an opportunity for positive political leadership on this issue has been lost.

Migrants, refugees and asylum seekers are not the only groups who have been identified as highlighting questions of identity and be-longing. The identities and allegiance of those who are of mixed descent, particularly those who have one white parent, have also attracted the interest of commentators reflecting on questions of national identity. Reactions to these individuals have often been somewhat polarised. Miscegenation and degeneration of the nation were seen as unfortunate consequences of migration by policy-makers in the mid-twentieth century (Parker and Song, 2001). Academic writing of the period focused on the ambiguous social status of such individuals and echoed popular concerns that children of mixed heritage were likely to have confused identities and feel un-certain as to where they belonged (Furedi, 2001).

At the same time, and to a greater degree in recent times, people of mixed heritage, particularly children, have been romanticised and portrayed as beautiful people, whose very existence embodies our multiculturalism. Citizens of mixed heritage are now officially recognised in the census categories. Yet they continue to be represented in the media, and in the popular imagination, both as a positive representation of multiculturalism and as the negative confirmation that cultural diversity inevitably implies conflicting loyalties and a loss of clear identity.

Citizenship is about a sense of belonging and also about political participation. At its most basic level, and symbolically, this includes the right to vote. We can teach the young about the right to vote, about the responsibilities attached to voting, and about the struggles which various groups have experienced, both in this country and in other countries, to claim this right. Nevertheless, the right to vote may feel less than adequate in a society where an individual or a family cannot enjoy basic security or freedom of movement because they are subject to racial harassment and violence in their home or on the streets. Similarly, the existence of institutional racism within British society serves to disadvantage certain groups in many areas, including education and employment. Notwithstanding government pledges to rid society of this problem, individuals are not yet able to exercise citizenship rights on the basis of equality.

In the face of discrimination and disadvantage many individuals from minority communities have demonstrated their determination to be active citizens, ready to transform their communities and enable the greater participation of others within society. For example, within the African Caribbean communities in Britain, supplementary schooling has been a key area of voluntary activity. Mirza and Reay (2000), in their study of black women's participation in supplementary schools, argue that, despite marginalisation and exclusion, these women are able to exercise citizenship in a way that society, and traditional discourse on citizenship, has overlooked. They argue that black women's 'acts of citizenship', as mothers and as teachers in supplementary schools, challenge the accepted dichotomy between the private and public spheres and reveal 'other ways of knowing' and 'other ways of being' a citizen (Mirza and Reay, 2000: 59). A number of black people, largely but not exclusively women, have also entered the teaching profession with the intention of making a difference to the lives of young people in their communities (Bryan *et al.*, 1985; Osler 1997a and 1997c). Their conscious efforts to enable others, both black and white, to overcome the disadvantage which they themselves have experienced, either as migrants whose qualifications were not recognised, or as students whose own schooling was inadequate, may also be viewed as acts of citizenship. These acts of citizenship serve to remind us, that for many people, not only is the distinction between the public and the private a false one, but so too is the distinction between the voluntary and the professional.

Supplementary schooling has also been a key area of voluntary activity within Asian communities, focusing 'on the linguistic, religious and cultural needs of the community which are often neglected by the state system' (Ohri, 2002). Ohri points out that such supplementary schools can contribute to young people's sense of belonging in their immediate communities. Such schools may also support the development of emotional ties with their parents' countries of origin and a broader understanding of development issues. Supplementary schooling is thus not only an act of citizenship, it also has the potential to contribute to the education for cosmopolitan citizenship, and enable young people to understand broader political issues and to participate at all levels from the local to the international.

Debates about British, or more usually, English identity, have revealed some confusion about what it means to be British and/or English. It would appear that English identity is particularly exclusive. Migrants to the USA can become American, and despite the continuing existence of racism in American society, it would appear that anyone can, in principle, become American. It is a citizenship marked by its great variety. It is perhaps harder to become British, and almost impossible for some people, even if they are born in England, to count as English. Whereas most people can recognise the concept of black British (even if they would prefer not to differentiate in that way), or black Londoner or black Liverpudlian, the concept of black English is to many a contradiction in terms. People of mixed descent may be expected to choose: either they can 'pass' as white and therefore are often expected to select this option and not draw attention to any other heritage, or they are not seen as English and may be told that they 'don't look English'.

The presence of minority groups serves to remind us that the exercise of citizenship rights implies more than formal legal citizenship status. Democracy implies more than democratic processes, practices and procedures, it also implies freedom from discrimination. For all citizens to feel a sense of belonging, they need to be able to exercise their rights on the basis of equality. An inclusive democracy needs laws protecting minorities from discrimination. It also needs to develop a human rights culture, in which individuals can feel secure and exercise their rights in an atmosphere free from discrimination. Citizenship implies a sense of belonging and that sense of belonging requires a sense of security and genuine inclusion. This sense of belonging cannot be taught to newcomers, nor can it be realised through a ceremony of belonging, it needs to be experienced

Making connections: education for cosmopolitan citizenship

Globalisation and increased interdependence now mean that organisations, people and events over which we may have little influence effect our everyday lives. The terrorist attacks of 11 September 2001 and their on-going consequences have made it impossible to avoid this reality. As we have argued in chapter two, preparing young people to participate as cosmopolitan citizens, capable of shaping the future of their own communities and of engaging in democratic processes at all levels, has become an urgent task. The nation state is no longer the only locus for democracy. The challenge is to develop democratic processes at all levels from the global to the local. The Social Forum at Porto Alegre in Brazil in 2002 provides just one example of ways in which international NGOs and local community groups are seeking to shape the future processes of globalisation. At the same time, individuals practise citizenship within local contexts. Whether engaged in democratic processes at local, national or international levels, citizens need skills that will enable them to participate and live together in contexts of diversity. In this final section we explore how we might draw on human rights as the basis for education in cosmopolitan citizenship which will prepare young people to live together in an interdependent world and to take responsibility for shaping that world.

Education for cosmopolitan citizenship is not a process that will be completed at school – it will extend beyond the school, into the community, with learners encouraged to make connections between their experiences and learning in the school and in the community. Just as citizenship itself is a lifelong process, so education for cosmopolitan citizenship is, necessarily, lifelong. Learners will require skills and attitudes which allow them to make connections between different contexts and situations, and to respond to constant change. Not only will learners need to apply this in schools and in local communities to national, regional and international contexts, they will also have to be able to make connections between these contexts. The greatest challenge that cosmopolitan citizens face is being able to make connections, to critique and to evaluate within contexts of cultural diversity.

This requires 'new ways of knowing' and a recognition that there are more 'ways of being' a citizen than have perhaps previously been recognised. Local citizenship, national citizenship, regional citizenship (such as European citizenship) and global citizenship are not necessarily in tension. So, for example, global citizenship does not mean asking individuals to reject their national citizenship or to accord it a lower status. Education for cosmopolitan citizenship must necessarily be about enabling learners to make connections between their immediate contexts and the global context; it encompasses citizenship learning as a whole. It implies a broader understanding of national identity; it requires recognition that British identity, for example, may be experienced differently by different people. It also implies recognition of our common humanity and a sense of solidarity with others. It is insufficient, however, to feel and express a sense of solidarity with others elsewhere, if we cannot establish a sense of solidarity with others in our own communities, especially those others whom we perceive to be different from ourselves. The challenge is to accept shared responsibility for our common future and for solving our common problems.

As we argued in chapter two, solidarity with others, and respect for others' cultures does not imply a radical relativism; we must stand somewhere, since '[it] is not possible to stand nowhere' (Figueroa, 2000: 55). Respect for others and for others' cultures implies critical respect, which in turn implies that we have some agreed reference points. It also implies an understanding of the roots of our own worldview, a recognition that our perceptions have been shaped both by our personal biographies and societal history. Education for cosmopolitan citizenship therefore requires an understanding of history and biography. Consequently, any programme for education for cosmopolitan citizenship will have both structural/political elements and personal and cultural elements (see Osler and Starkey, 1996).

We have stressed the structural and political elements of citizenship learning in chapter two, arguing that a politically literate citizen will need to understand and engage in processes of change at all levels, including the global. Political literacy does not only imply an understanding of rights, democratic processes and institutions. It also implies the skills to operate in intercultural contexts, and this, inevitably, requires a confidence in one's own culture and worldview. This does not mean that this worldview is forever fixed; it is necessarily provisional. Similarly, all cultures are dynamic and subject to change. Our judgements do not change by whim, but when new evidence is presented which requires a re-assessment of our original position. Educational experiences may provide opportunities for reflection and re-assessment. Language learning, for example:

> can provide the means of decentring, and the critical cultural awareness which allows learners to reflect critically on their own society and their own values, meanings and behaviours within it (Byram and Guilherme, 2000: 63).

The cosmopolitan citizen needs to be confident in his or her own identities and requires learning opportunities to explore and develop them. To neglect the personal and cultural aspects of citizenship is to ignore the issue of belonging. As we have argued, citizenship requires a sense of belonging. Without such a sense it is unlikely that individuals will be able to contribute or achieve what Braithwaite referred to as 'full responsible citizenship'.

How then can we educate cosmopolitan citizens so that they are able to recognise our common humanity, make connections between their own lives and those of others, operating in contexts of cultural diversity and change? We suggested in chapter one that cosmopolitan citizens need to acquire the skills of intercultural evaluation (Hall, 2000; Parekh, 2000b). Human rights provide us with a set of internationally agreed principles, as formulated in such internationally agreed texts, such as the Universal Declaration of Human Rights (UDHR) and the 1989 UN Convention on the Rights of the Child (CRC), against which we can make critical assessments.

We suggest that such texts provide us with a framework from which a school or any other learning community can derive a set of explicit, shared values. These texts provide us with a set of principles against which we can critically reflect on our own culture, values, beliefs and behaviours and those of our fellow citizens. Such reflection may enable us to understand more fully the ways in which our own worldview is historically and biographically situated. From such a reference point it becomes possible to respect others and their cultures, while not necessarily accepting all aspects of another culture. Human rights do not provide a set of clear-cut rules but rather general principles. It is therefore possible to recognise that these principles might be secured and upheld within a variety of cultural contexts, by different means.

Verhellen (2000) has usefully developed a model of children's rights, distinguishing between rights *to, in* and *through* education. All young people have a right *to* education, outlined in the UDHR and confirmed in the Convention on the Rights of the Child. This right provides for equal access for all. School systems which systematically disadvantage or discriminate or exclude any group of children, whether on the basis of ethnicity, gender or class, are in contravention of the Convention. Phenomena such as truancy, exclusion or denial of the right of free access are examples of failure to secure the right to education. Rights in education are the right to express an opinion; freedom of expression; freedom of thought, conscience and religion; freedom of association; and protection of privacy. These are rights that are more likely to be guaranteed if they have been addressed by the school leadership (Osler and Starkey, 1998; Cunningham, 2000). In chapter two (figure 2.3) we presented a model of a human rights school, built on the principles of democracy, transparency and inclusion. The model illustrates rights in education, but it also draws our attention to the need for human rights education, or rights through education, so that young people are aware of their rights. Students' rights in education are more likely to be upheld if there is also provision of rights through education. In other words, familiarity with rights is the best guarantee against infringement.

Rights through education are critical to cosmopolitan citizenship. Human rights education provides young people with a set of principles which are the basis for intercultural evaluation. Learning communities built on human rights principles, which uphold rights in education, also provide a model of human rights and the experience of human rights. Education for cosmopolitan citizenship, founded on human rights, will enable learners to recognise our common humanity and provide a sense of belonging to a global community. Citizens will have opportunities to express solidarity with those whose rights are infringed; opportunities to exercise their rights to participation; and the skills to do this within contexts of cultural diversity.

Appendix 1:
Global education questionnaire

The questions address a range of individuals including policy-makers, ministry officials, local and regional education authorities, and NGOs. Please answer as many as you can. Some may not apply to you. We are interested both **in factual information and in your personal opinions and perspectives**. We also welcome supporting **policy documents and examples**. Unfortunately we do not have the resources to translate materials. All documents and summaries should therefore be in ENGLISH.

1. Are you aware of any **official policies or guidance from the Ministry of Education** relating to Global Education (including citizenship education [civics], education for sustainable development, environmental education, intercultural/multicultural education, education for human rights and peace)? Please list these, indicating their formal status and date of publication. Where possible, send examples.

2. Do any **other Ministries** support initiatives to promote GE in schools? For example, do they provide resources, guidelines or materials? Please explain and, if possible, provide supporting documentation.

3. In what ways does the Government support **international initiatives** to promote GE? For example, is anything done to support and encourage schools to join international networks and links such as UNESCO's Associated Schools Project? How does the Government inform schools of GE-related statements of the Council of Europe's Council of Ministers?

4. Do **regional or local authorities** set policies or support GE? (eg. policies on human rights education or intercultural education?) What is the status of these initiatives? Is there a wide divergence of practice between different regions?

5. Where and how are the various component parts of GE referred to in the **primary and secondary curriculum**? For example, in any statement of values or subject content?

6. Give **examples of GE in schools** and of any recent projects, materials or events which support global dimensions in the curriculum? How do teachers access **resources** or information about resources? Give examples.

7. What guidelines or legislation exist relating to the various component parts of GE in **initial teacher training**? What is the formal status of these documents and to which student teachers do these apply (primary, secondary)?

8. Are these opportunities for teachers to participate in **in-service training** in aspects of GE? Are these mandatory or optional? Please give examples and providers.

9. Are there non-governmental organisation **(NGO) networks or platforms** at regional or national levels on the global dimensions of education for democratic citizenship, sustainable development, human rights, etc.? Give examples.

10. What are the GE **roles and activities of NGOs** in schools and teacher training? Do you know of examples of international school-focused NGO projects?

11. Are you aware of any **academic research** in this area? Please name any research centres devoted to GE. Give examples of any GE **publications** aimed at researchers, teacher trainers or teachers.

12. What do you see as the strengths, weaknesses, opportunities and threats (**SWOT**) to GE and its component parts in your country?

Thank you for taking the time to answer these questions.

Bibliography

Alibhai Brown, Y. (2000) *After Multiculturalism.* London: Foreign Policy Centre.

Amnesty International (2001) *September 11 Crisis Response Guide: human rights education program for junior and high schools.* New York: Amnesty International USA.

Barber, M. (1996) *The Learning Game: arguments for an education revolution.* London: Victor Gollancz.

Beck, U. (2000) *What is Globalisation?* Cambridge: Polity Press in association with Blackwell.

Beck, U. (2001) The fight for a cosmopolitan future. *New Statesman:* 5 November, 33-34.

Boland, T. (1999) *Primary Education in the Netherlands.* Enschede: Netherlands Institute for Curriculum Development.

Brennan, F. (1994) A development education project in Irish primary schools, in: A. Osler (Ed.) *Development Education: global perspectives in the curriculum.* London: Cassell.

Bron, J.G. (2001) *Mensenrechten door het curriculum (Human Rights through the curriculum).* Enschede: SLO.

Bryan, B., Dadzie, S. and Scafe, S. (1985) *The Heart of the Race: Black women's lives in Britain.* London: Virago.

Buttenschon, C. (1998) *The United Nations Association and Education.* Copenhagen: Danish United Nations Association.

Byram, M., and Guilherme, M. (2000) Human rights, cultures and language teaching, in: A. Osler (Ed.) *Citizenship and Democracy in Schools: diversity, identity, equality.* Stoke: Trentham.

Calvert, R. (2001) Meeting the challenge of creating real understanding, *The Development Education Journal,* 7 (2): 22-23.

Cantle, T. (2001) *Community Cohesion.* Report of the Independent Review Team. London: Home Office. www.homeoffice.gov.uk

Carter, C. (2000) Meeting the challenge of inclusion: human rights education to improve relationships in a boys' secondary school, in: A. Osler (Ed.) *Citizenship and Democracy in Schools: diversity, identity, equality.* Stoke: Trentham.

Carter, C., Harber, C., and Serf, J. (2002) *Towards Ubuntu: critical teacher education and citizenship.* Birmingham: Development Education Centre.

Carter, C., and Osler, A. (2000) Human rights, identities and conflict management: a study of school culture as experienced through classroom relationships. *Cambridge Journal of Education,* 30 (3): 335-356.

Council of Europe (1985) Recommendation R (85) 7 of the Committee of Ministers to Member States on Teaching and Learning about Human Rights in Schools, reprinted in: A. Osler and H. Starkey *Teacher Education and Human Rights*. London: David Fulton.

Council of Europe (1993) *Vienna Declaration*. 9 October. Strasbourg: Council of Europe.

Cunningham, J. (2000) Democratic practice in a secondary school, in: A. Osler (Ed.) *Citizenship and Democracy in Schools: diversity, identity, equality.* Stoke: Trentham.

Danish Ministry of Education (1995) *Act on the Folkeskole, the Danish Primary and Secondary School.* Copenhagen: Danish Ministry of Education. www.uvm.dk/ eng/publications/laws/actonthe.htm.

Danish Ministry of Education (1997) *The Administration of the Folkeskole.* Copenhagen: Danish Ministry of Education.

Danish Ministry of Education (1998) *The International Dimension on the Subjects and Themes of the Folkeskole.* Copenhagen: Danish Ministry of Education.

Danish Ministry of Education (2001) *News: The New Government.* www.uvm.dk /eng/news/newgov.htm.

Davies, L. and Kirkpatrick, G. (2000) *The Eurodem Project: a review of pupil democracy in Europe.* London: Children's Rights Alliance.

Department for Education and Employment (1999) *DfEE News 272/99,* 16 June.

Department for Education and Employment (2000) *Developing a Global Dimension in the School Curriculum.* 0115/2000 London: DfEE.

Department for Education and Science (2000) *Major Expansion of Visiting Teacher Service for Traveller Children.* Press release September 2000. Dublin: DES.

Department for Education and Science (2001) *The Allocation of Teachers to Second Level Schools, report of the expert group to the Minister for Education and Science.* Dublin: DES.

Department for Education and Science (undated) *A Brief Description of the Irish Education System.* Dublin: DES. www.irlgov.ie/educ.

Department for Education and Skills (2001) *Schools Achieving Success.* White Paper. London: DfES. www.dfes.gov.uk/achievingsuccess.

Department for International Development (1997) *Eliminating World Poverty: a challenge for the 21st century.* White Paper. London: DFID.

Department for International Development (1999) *Building Support for Development: strategy paper* 4/99 1K. London: DFID Information Department.

Department for International Development (2000) *Eliminating World Poverty: making globalisation work for the poor.* White Paper. London: DFID.

Department for International Development (2000) *Enabling Effective Support: development education in schools, consultation for action.* London: DFID Information Department. www.dfid.gov.uk.

Department of Education and Science (1995) *Charting our Education Future.* Dublin: DES.

Department of Environment and Local Government (2001) *Towards Sustainable Local Communities. Guidelines on Local Agenda 21.* Dublin: Department of Environment and Local Government.

Department of Foreign Affairs (1996) *Challenges and Opportunities Abroad.* Dublin: Department of Foreign Affairs.

Department of Foreign Affairs (undated) Information Facts. Economic Development. Dublin: Department of Foreign Affairs. www.gov.ie/iveagh/

Department of Justice, Equality and Law Reform (2001) *Minister Formally Establishes the Human Rights Commission.* Press release, 25 July 2001. Dublin: DJELR.

Department of the Environment, Transport and the Regions (2001) *Education for Sustainable Development: more relevant than ever. The third annual report of the Sustainable Development Education Panel.* London: DETR.

Department of the Taoiseach (2001) Speech by Mr Bertie Ahern at the launch of the Government's Anti-Racism Programme, 24 October 2001. Dublin: Department of the Taoisearch.

Development Education Association (1998) *Training Teachers for Tomorrow.* London: DEA.

Development Education Association (1999) *A Framework for the International Dimension for Schools in England.* London: DEA.

Development Education Association (2000) *Principles and Practice for Development Education Practitioners Working with Schools.* London: DfID.

Development Education Association (2001) *Citizenship Education: the global dimension. Guidance for key stages 3 and 4.* London: DEA.

Development Education Association (2002) *Improving Practice in Development Education series – case studies in global perspectives in initial teacher education and training.* London: DEA.

Development Education Association (undated) *The Challenge of the Global Society: development education in the 21st Century.* London: DEA internet document.

Development Education Centre (1998) *Forward Thinking: the review 1.* Birmingham: DEC.

Development Education Centre (1999) *Forward Thinking: the review 2.* Birmingham: DEC.

Development Education Centre (2000a) *Forward Thinking: the review 3.* Birmingham: DEC.

Development Education Centre (2000b) *Learning Today with Tomorrow in Mind, sustainable development education: the report.* Birmingham: DEC.

Development Education Centre (undated) *Forward Thinking: broadening young people's world view.* Birmingham: Development Education Centre and LEA.

Dudley, J. and Harvey, P. (2001) *Control of Immigration: statistics 2001* 22, 14/01. www.homeoffice.gov.uk/rds/pdfs/hosb1401.pdf.

Dummett, A. (1973) *A Portrait of English Racism.* Harmondsworth: Penguin.

Eggleston , J., Dunn, D. K., and Anjali, M. (1986) *Education for Some: the educational and vocational experiences of 15-18-year-old members of ethnic minority groups*. Stoke: Trentham.

Eurobarometer 50.1 (1999) *Europeans and Development Aid*. Brussels: for the European Commission. www.social-science-gesis.de/en/data_service/eurobarometer.

Eurydice (2000a) *The Education System in Denmark*. www.eurydice.org.Eurybase/Application/eurybase.htm.

Eurydice (2000b) *The Education System in the Netherlands*. www.eurydice.org/Eurybase/Application/eurybase.htm.

Figueroa, P. (2000) Citizenship education for a plural society, in: A. Osler (Ed.) *Citizenship and Democracy in Schools: diversity, identity, equality*. Stoke: Trentham.

Fryer, P. (1984) *Staying Power: the history of black people in Britain*. London: Pluto Press.

Furedi, F. (2001) How sociology imagined 'mixed race', in: D. Parker and M. Song (Eds.) *Re-thinking 'Mixed Race'*. London: Pluto Press.

Gannon, M. (2000) *Audit of Research: development education in Ireland 1990-2000*. Dublin: National Committee for Development Education.

Giddens, A. (2000) *Globalisation: good or bad?* www.globaldimensions.net/articles/debate/giddenstext.html.

Gill, B., Clifford, A., McCarthy, S., O'Shea, K., and Trant, A. (1999) *Education for Reconciliation: a curriculum investigation*. Dublin: Curriculum Development Unit.

Gillborn, D., and Gipps, C. (1996) *Recent Research on the Achievements of Ethnic Minority Pupils*. London: HMSO.

Gillborn, D., and Youdell, D. (2000) *Rationing Education: policy, practice, reform and equity*. Buckingham: Open University Press.

Gilroy, P. (2000) *Between Two Camps: nations, cultures and the allure of race*. London: Allen Lane, Penguin Press.

Gittens, I. (2000) The role of black governors, in: A. Osler (Ed.) *Citizenship and Democracy in Schools: diversity, identity, equality*. Stoke: Trentham.

Gray, J. (2001) The era of globalisation is over. *New Statesman*, 24 September, 25-27.

Hahn, C. L. (1999) Citizenship education: an empirical study of policy, practices and outcomes, *Oxford Review of Education*, 25 (1 and 2): 231-250.

Hall, S. (2000) Multicultural citizens: monocultural citizenship, in: N. Pearce and J. Hallgarten (Eds.) *Tomorrow's Citizens: critical debates in citizenship and education*. London: Institute for Public Policy Research.

Hammond, J., Looney, A., and McCarthy, S. (2001) *Education for Democratic Citizenship. The Development of EDC policy in the Republic of Ireland at lower post-primary level*. Strasbourg: Paper presented at the Council for Cultural Co-operation, 31 May.

Held, D. (1995) Democracy and the new international order, in: D. Archibugi and D. Held (Eds.) *Cosmopolitan Democracy*. Cambridge: Polity Press.

Held, D. (1996) *Models of Democracy.* 2nd edition. Cambridge: Polity Press.

Held, D. (2001) Violence and justice in a global age. www.opendemocracy.net/document_store/doc648-5.pdf.

Holden, C., and Clough, N. (1998) (Eds.) *Children as Citizens: education for participation in democracies old and new.* London: Jessica Kingsley.

Home Office (1999) *Stephen Lawrence Inquiry: Home Secretary's Action Plan.* London: Home Office.

Home Office (2002) *Secure Borders, Safe Haven: integration with diversity in modern Britain. White paper.* London: Home Office.

Hooghoff, H. (2001) *Developing a Global Dimension in Dutch Education.* Enschede: Netherlands Institute for Curriculum Development and the Consortium of Institutions for Research and Development in Education in Europe.

Igniateff, M. (2001) What will victory look like? *The Guardian,* 19 October, G2: 3-5.

Karsten, S. (1998) School autonomy in the Netherlands. The development of a new administrative layer. *Eduational Management and Administration,* 26 (4): 395-405.

Klein, G. (1992) *Education Towards Race Equality.* London: Cassell.

Korsgaard, O., Walters, S., and Anderson, R. (2001) (Eds.) *Learning for Democratic Citizenship.* Copenhagen: Association for World Citizenship and the Danish University of Education.

Koster, B. and Snoek, M. (1998) A National Curriculum for Teacher Education: a Dutch case study. *Journal of In-service Education,* 24 (3): 547-557.

Kragh, G. (1996) Education for democracy, social justice, respect for human rights and global responsibility: a psychological perspective, in: A. Osler, H.F. Rathenow and H. Starkey (Eds.) *Teaching for Citizenship in Europe.* Stoke: Trentham.

Larsen, N. (2000) *Action Competence between Individualisation and Globalisation.* Copenhagen: Royal Danish School for Educational Studies.

Larsen, N., Mogensen, F. and Moos, L. (1999) *Action 21: An Evaluation.* Copenhagen: Royal Danish School for Educational Studies.

Macpherson, W. *et al.* (1999) *The Stephen Lawrence Inquiry.* London: The Stationery Office.

Mahoney, P. (1998) Democracy and school leadership in England and Denmark. *British Journal of Educational Studies,* 46 (3): 302-317.

Malik, K. (2002) The real value of diversity, *Connections,* Winter 2001-2: 10-13.

Ministry of Foreign Affairs (1989) *The Dutch Constituion.* Ministry of Foreign Affairs. http://www.minbuza.nl./english/menu.asp?key=257783andPad-257570, 257574.

Mirza, H. S., and Reay, D. (2000) Redefining citizenship: Black women educators and 'the third space', in: M. Arnot and J. Dillabough (Eds.) *Challenging Democracy: international perspectives on gender, education and citizenship.* London: Routledgefalmer.

Muller, S., and Timm, L. (2001) Global education in Denmark: caught between two government departments, *Development Education Journal,* 7. (2): 31-32.

National Anti-Racism Awareness Project (2001) *Know Racism.* www.knowracism.ie.

National Committee for Development Education (1999) *Home and Away: a theme-based guide to development education resources for primary schools*. Dublin: NCDE.

Netherlands Ministry of Education, Culture and Science (1991) *Widening Horizons*. Zoetermeer: Ministry of Education, Culture and Science.

Netherlands Ministry of Education, Culture and Science (1997) *Unbounded Talent*. Zoetermeer: Ministry of Education, Culture and Science.

Netherlands Ministry of Education, Culture and Science (1998a) *Unbounded Talent Action Plan*. Zoetermeer: Ministry of Education, Culture and Science.

Netherlands Ministry of Education, Culture and Science (1998b) *Attainment Targets 1998-2003. Basic Education in the Netherlands*. Zoetermeer: Ministry of Education, Culture and Science, www.minocw.nl/english/index.html.

Netherlands Ministry of Education, Culture and Science 1998c) *Education in the Netherlands*. Zoetermeer: Ministry of Education, Culture and Science.

Netherlands Ministry of Education, Culture and Science (2000) *Knowledge: give and take. Internationalisation of education in the Netherlands*. Zoetermeer: Ministry of Education, Culture and Science.

Netherlands Ministry of the Interior (1983) Netherlands Constitution. The Hague: Ministry of the Interior. www.uni-wuerzburg.de/law/nl00000_.html.

Ohri, A. (1997) *The World in Our Neighbourhood: black and ethnic minority communities and development education*. London: Development Education Association.

Ohri, A. (2002) Identity and contribution to development, *Development Education Journal*, 8 (2): 22-24.

O'Loughlin, E., Quigley, P. and Wegimont, L. (2000) *Irish Attitudes Towards Overseas Development: challenges for a research agenda*. Dublin: DEFY.

Organisation for Economic Co-operation and Development (2001a) *Economic Survey Of Ireland*. Paris: OECD.

Organisation for Economic Co-operation and Development (2001b) *OECD in Figures. Statistics on the Member Countries*. Paris: OECD, www.oecd.org.

Osborn, M. (1999) National context, educational goals and pupil experience of schooling and learning in three European countries. *Compare*, 29 (3): 287-301.

Oscarsson, V. (1996) Pupils' views of the future, in: A. Osler, H.F. Rathenow and H. Starkey (Eds.) *Teaching for Citizenship in Europe*. Stoke: Trentham.

Osler, A. (1997a) *The Education and Careers of Black Teachers: changing identities, changing lives*. Buckingham: Open University Press.

Osler, A. (1997b) *Exclusion from School and Racial Equality: research report*. London: Commission for Racial Equality.

Osler, A. (1997c) Black teachers and citizenship: researching differing identities, *Teachers and Teaching: theory and practice*, 3 (1) 47-60.

Osler, A. (1999) Citizenship, democracy and political literacy. *Multicultural Teaching*, 18 (1): 12-15 and 29.

Osler, A. (2000a) (Ed.) *Citizenship and Democracy in Schools: diversity, identity, equality*. Stoke: Trentham.

Osler, A. (2000b) Children's rights, responsibilities and understandings of school discipline. *Research Papers in Education*, 15 (1): 49-67.

Osler, A. (2000c) The Crick Report: difference, equality and racial justice. *The Curriculum Journal*, 11 (1): 25-37.

Osler, A. (2001) *Teachers Changing Lives: survival, success, subversion*, University of Leicester, School of Education, Occasional Paper 2.

Osler, A. (2002) Achieving race equality in education: legal duties, inspections and institutional responses. *Development Education Journal*, 8 (2): 7-10.

Osler, A., and Morrison, M. (2000) *Inspecting Schools for Race Equality: OFSTED's strengths and weaknesses*. Stoke: Trentham for the Commission for Racial Equality.

Osler, A., Rathenow, H.F., and Starkey, H. (1996) (Eds.) *Teaching for Citizenship in Europe*. Stoke: Trentham.

Osler, A., and Starkey, H. (1996) *Teacher Education and Human Rights*. London: David Fulton.

Osler, A., and Starkey, H. (1998) Children's rights and citizenship: some implications for the management of schools. *International Journal of Children's Rights*, 6: 313-333.

Osler, A., and Starkey, H. (2000) Citizenship, human rights and cultural diversity, in: A. Osler (Ed.) *Citizenship and democracy in Schools: diversity, identity, equality*. Stoke: Trentham.

Osler, A., and Starkey, H. (2001a) Young People in Leicester (UK): community, identity and citizenship. *Interdialogos*, 2 (01): 48-49.

Osler, A , and Starkey, H. (2001b) Legal perspectives on values, culture and education: human rights, responsibilities and values in education, in: J. Cairns, D. Lawton and R. Gardner (Eds.) *Values, Culture and Education: World Yearbook of Education*. London: Kogan Page.

Osler, A., and Starkey, H. (2002a) Education for citizenship: mainstreaming the fight against racism? *European Journal of Education*, 37 (2).

Osler, A., and Starkey, H. (2002b forthcoming) Young people as cosmopolitan citizens, in F. Audigier and N. Fink (Eds.) *Learning to Live Together*. Geneva: International Bureau of Education.

Parekh, B. (2000a) *The Future of Multi-Ethnic Britain*. London: Profile Books, for the Runnymede Trust/ Commission on the Future of Multi-Ethnic Britain.

Parekh, B. (2000b) *Rethinking Multiculturalism: cultural diversity and political theory*. London: Macmillan.

Parker, D., and Song, M. (2001) Introduction, in: D. Parker and M. Song (Eds.) *Rethinking 'Mixed Race'*. London: Pluto Press.

Parkin, J. (2000) *Young People, the Media and Popular Culture*. Dublin: Development Education for Youth.

Qualifications and Curriculum Authority (1998) *Education for Citizenship and the Teaching of Democracy in Schools*. Crick Report. London: QCA.

Richardson, R. (1979) (Ed.) *Learning for Change in World Society: reflections, activities and resources*. London: World Studies Project.

Richardson, R. (1997) (Ed.) *Islamophobia: a challenge for us all.* London: Runnymede Trust.

Richardson, R., and Wood, A. (1999) *Inclusive Schools, Inclusive Society: race and identity on the agenda.* Stoke: Trentham Books.

Richie, D. (2001) *One Oldham: one future.* Oldham Independent Review Panel Report. www.oldhamir.org.uk.

Ruane, B., Horgan, K. and Cremin, P. (1999) *The World in the Classroom: development education in the primary curriculum.* Limerick: Curriculum Development Unit, Mary Immaculate College of Education.

Sinclair, S. (2000) Defining development awareness. *Developments* DFID, 11: 13.

Skole og Samfund (2002) *The Danish School Parents' Association.* www.skolesamfund.dk/eng.

Starkey, H. (1994) Development education and human rights education, in: A. Osler (Ed.) *Development Education: global perspectives in the curriculum.* London: Cassell.

Teacher Training Agency (2000) *Raising the attainment of minority ethnic pupils: guidance and resource materials for providers of initial teacher training.* London: Teacher Training Agency.

Tennant, G. (2001) The Model United Nations General Assembly Project. *Teaching Citizenship,* 1 (2): 34-37.

Thalhammer, E., Zucha, V., Enzenhofer, E., Salfinger, B., and Ogris, G. (2001) *Attitudes Towards Minority Groups in the European Union: a special analysis of the Eurobarometer survey.* Vienna: European Monitoring Centre on Racism and Xenophobia.

Tomlinson, S. (1993) The multicultural task group: the group that never was, in: A. King and M. Reiss (Eds.) *The Multicultural Dimension of the National Curriculum.* London: Falmer.

Torney-Purta, J., Lehmann, R., Oswald, H., and Schulz, W. (2001) *Citizenship and Education in Twenty-Eight Countries: civic knowledge and engagement at age fourteen.* Amsterdam: International Association for the Evaluation of Educational Achievement.

United Nations Educational Scientific and Cultural Organisation (1995) *Declaration and Integrated Framework of Action on Education for Peace, Human Rights and Democracy.* Paris: UNESCO.

United Nations Educational Scientific and Cultural Organisation (2000) *Fifth Session of the Advisory Committee on Education for Peace, Human Rights, Democracy, International Understanding and Tolerance: final report.* ED-2000/CONF. 501, 25 March. Paris: UNESCO.

Verhellen, E. (2000) Children's rights and education, in: A. Osler (Ed.) *Citizenship and Democracy in Schools: diversity, identity, equality.* Stoke: Trentham.

Wegimont, L. (Ed) (2000) *Development and Justice Issues: Irish Attitudes. A Survey of Irish public attitudes towards a range of development issues, local and global.* Dublin: Development Education for Youth.

Wegimont, L. (2001) Personal communication, May 2001.

INDEX